025395-2 √92 f

D1389724

Ⓕ

CLASSIC TEXTILE
DESIGNS

CLASSIC TEXTILE
DESIGNS

M. DUPONT-AUBERVILLE

FIFTY PLATES, IN GOLD, SILVER AND COLOURS
COMPRISING UPWARDS OF 1,000 VARIOUS STYLES
OF ANCIENT, MEDIÆVAL AND MODERN DESIGNS
OF TEXTILE FABRICS WITH EXPLANATORY
DESCRIPTIONS AND A GENERAL INTRODUCTION.

FOREWORD BY
JENNIFER HARRIS

WHITWORTH ART GALLERY
MANCHESTER

BRACKEN BOOKS

LONDON

Previously published as *L'Ornement des Tissus* in Paris by
Ducher & Cie
and as *Ornamental Textile Fabrics* in London by
Asher & Co., 1877

This edition published 1989 by Bracken Books
an imprint of Bestseller Publications Ltd.
Princess House, 50 Eastcastle Street
London W1N 7AP, England

Copyright © Bracken Books 1989

ISBN 1 85170 278 4

Printed and bound in Hong Kong

FOREWORD

M. Dupont-Auberville's classic work *L'Ornement des Tissus* was published in French in 1877, at a period when interest in historic ornament was at its height. The book was translated into English as *Ornamental Textile Fabrics* and published in London the same year, where its appeal would have been, if anything, even greater; for British textile design in the second half of the nineteenth century is characterised above all by the revival of interest in historic patterns and by their imaginative reworking in the creation of new designs. All the leading designers of the period sought and found their inspiration in the past. Although some, like William Morris, might have studied early textiles first-hand in the newly-formed collections of the South Kensington Museum (now the Victoria and Albert), the majority almost certainly relied on the anthologies of historic ornament which were being produced in increasing numbers from the 1870s onwards. Like Owen Jones' highly influential *Grammar of Ornament* (1856), works such as Dupont-Auberville's volume of historic textile patterns and Friedrich Fischbach's *Ornamente der Gewebe* (*Pattern in Textiles*), which was published during the same period (1874–8), were in effect encyclopaedias of ornamental design and helped to make decoration a respectable academic study. They were widely used by students of architecture and the applied arts, and would have been found in the libraries of most free-lance designers and in the design studios of large manufacturers throughout the late nineteenth and early twentieth centuries.

The style and presentation of Dupont-Auberville's encyclopaedia of designs takes its inspiration from Owen Jones' work, but differs from it in concentrating exclusively on ornamental textiles of mainly European origin. The author assembled an impressive catalogue of characteristic pattern types of the thirteenth to eighteenth centuries, which serves as one of the earliest histories of European textiles. Inevitably, modern scholarship has revealed a number of errors in his dating and attribution of patterns: several of the plates attributed to the seventeenth century are, in fact, examples dating from the early eighteenth century. This is hardly surprising, since the book was compiled at a time when historic textiles were only just beginning to be collected and properly documented, and such historical inaccuracies in no way detract from the work's intrinsic value as a source book for historic ornament. The large number of profusely illustrated plates makes the book a rich source of inspiration for designers, as well as a classic work of reference of pattern types for everyone with an interest in the subject of textile design.

While Modernism reigned supreme in the 1920s and 1930s the decorative tradition was cast aside, and the great encyclopaedias of ornamental design were taken off the library shelves. Ornamental qualities in design were dismissed as trivial and the vocabulary of ornament – palmettes, fleurons, diapers – forgotten. In the last two decades, however, historic ornament has been 're-discovered' as a visual language and the decorative arts are once again flourishing. Today, this handsome new edition of Dupont-Auberville's book will be welcomed not only as an impressive record of a time when interest in decoration was at its apogee, but also as a source of new ideas by those designers and manufacturers who are again seeking their inspiration in the art and design of the past; for we live in a period which exhibits a fascination with history almost as strong as that of the late Victorians. The introduction to the first French edition of this book opened with a quotation from La Fontaine which can just as easily be applied to the 1980s as to the 1870s:

> We know not how to surpass the achievements of our ancestors; the only glory we are left with is that of following in their footsteps or of imitating them.

Jennifer Harris
Curator of Textiles
Whitworth Art Gallery
University of Manchester

ORNAMENTAL TEXTILE FABRICS

OF

ALL NATIONS AND EPOCHS.

INTRODUCTION.

A FONTAINE has remarked that "we can scarcely hope to surpass the ancients, who have left us nothing but the glory of following in their footsteps," a statement which, if true of literature, is even more so of the Art we are about to describe and illustrate under the title of ORNAMENTAL TEXTILE FABRICS.

Thousands of years before our era the Indians, Egyptians, Assyrians, and Phœnicians wove plain stuffs as fine and delicate as those produced in our modern workshops; nor were they less skilled in the production of fancy materials, often adorned by them with exceedingly ingenious designs. Such embellishments must doubtless have begun with simple needlework and embroidery.

Amongst the Jews the Mosaic law required the sacred vestments to be enriched with embroidered ornaments, though such display is restricted by the Prophet Ezekiel to the Sanctuary. He reproaches the women of his time for wearing garments overdone with embroidery. On the other hand, the good wife in the last chapter of Proverbs is praised for her knowledge of this art. " She seeketh wool, and flax," says the inspired writer, " and worketh willingly with her hands . . . . She layeth her hands to the spindle, and her hands hold the distaff . . . . all her household are clothed with scarlet. She maketh herself coverings of tapestry; her clothing is silk and purple . . . . She maketh fine linen, and selleth it; and delivereth girdles unto the merchant."

Amongst the Assyrians also the monuments of Khorsabad show that embroideries of great delicacy and wrought with gold thread of the highest price were displayed on the robes of persons of distinction. The same practice prevailed in Egypt, India, Persia, China, in a word, wherever civilization found a footing. We know that the Babylonians excelled in the art of embroidery, and it was at Babylon that were produced those marvellous coverings for the couches set apart for the guests at the banquets, and which are said to have cost as much as £32,000!

The Homeric heroines, Helen, Penelope, Calypso, Circe, and so many others are represented as employed at needlework, and are constantly mentioned by the poet in connection with their woollen stuffs and their spindles.

From what has been said it is evident that the art of ornamenting textile fabrics was one of the earliest of human inventions. Traces of it are met with even amongst the least industrial races. Each people naturally employed such materials as were available to them. In the absence of silk, which continued so long to be the exclusive monopoly of China, and which did not find its way to Egypt till the second or third century before our era, thence spreading throughout the West, cotton, linen, hemp, wool, gold and silver thread sufficed, in skilful hands, to carry the art of embroidery to a pitch of perfection never afterwards surpassed. We have reason to believe that the cotton and linen fabrics of the Egyptians and Babylonians were not a whit inferior to what these nations might have made with silk, which, notwithstanding what has been said to the contrary, was wholly unknown to them.

Hence the Jews, migrating from Egypt and deriving their costly materials from that country, had no knowledge of any but cotton and linen stuffs, though a wrong rendering of the Hebrew word *shesh* (Exod., Chap. xxvi.) has led to the belief that silk was amongst the rich materials ordered by Moses to be used for the inner "vail" of the Tabernacle.

Nevertheless, silk existed in China upwards of three thousand years before our era. This material had already been in use some three hundred years in that country, when the Empress *Si-Ling-Chi* discovered the means of imparting to the costly thread its full and natural gloss and elasticity. Some centuries later on the Chinese historians show us the Emperor *Chun* traversing his vast dominions, and at the foot of Mount *Taï* receiving the homage of his numerous vassals, who present him with such things as are most likely to please him—silk and woollen tissues, raw silk, and fabrics of divers colours. At that remote period the manufacture of silk had already made considerable progress, the richest dyes being skilfully employed to enhance the brilliancy of materials rendered doubly valuable by means of fine embroidery.

Long after this event, some twelve centuries before the Christian era, when the Chinese Empire was split up into a number of feudal states, we read that all the feudatory courts of the Empire vied with each other in the splendour of their costumes, and surrounded themselves with the most skilled artisans in the manufacture of silken stuffs. It also appears that about nine hundred years before our era, the Emperor *Li-Wang* wore robes of gold brocade sumptuously adorned.

The choicest materials were woven under the eyes of the Emperor, and in the very palace itself. The learned author of the history of silk, M. Pariset, thence concludes that they were reserved for the magnates of the Empire; but we would prefer to suppose that the Chinese sovereign merely wished thereby to foster an industry for which he foresaw a splendid future.

It may be asked, how such an industrious country as Egypt failed forthwith to avail itself of the valuable Chinese discovery. This was partly due to the jealous and suspicious disposition of the Chinese people, who for a long time shut themselves out from all communication with the West. Hence even if silk was at that period manufactured in sufficient quantity for exportation, it would have found no outlet for foreign trade. Some few Jews after the dispersion may, doubtless, have penetrated as far as China, and there procured silken fabrics. These materials, however, never found their way very far westwards, and in any case no regular trade can have been established between Egypt and the Celestial Empire.

The eastern Asiatic nations alone were acquainted with this Chinese product, as is evident from the universal tradition, which refers to a common origin the ornamental types and patterns of those peoples. Nowhere did the reverence for this tradition make itself more vividly felt than in the East, where, with all the corruption and change of taste, the fundamental decorative designs ever preserved their original stamp. Hence, whatever may be said to the contrary, we do not think we are going too far in saying that the eastern peoples copied from age to age the inspirations they first received from China.

Egypt was fain to rest satisfied with the materials produced on her own soil, including linen, cotton, and wool. The Egyptians were also acquainted with certain worms that spun a thread adapted to the manufacture of a silky but insubstantial fabric. Hence the current misconceptions regarding the true mulberry silk-worm.

Before the cotton plant reached the fertile valley of the Nile, Egypt imported the cotton of India in large quantities, employing it for the manufacture of those " fringed and blue striped girdles, figured fabrics, striped cloths, plushes, and velveteens," still found wrapped round the mummies, and so many curious specimens of which may be seen in the public museums.

It is therefore evident that the Egyptians manufactured their textile fabrics of linen, wool, and cotton alone. Pliny (*Hist. Nat.*, Lib. XIX., Chap. II., III., IV., V., VI.) speaks of no other materials, and we know that cotton was reserved for the priests and burials, linen being more especially used for secular purposes and fancy articles. Herodotus speaks of linen cuirasses, woven of marvellously fine threads; and in his *Voyage en Egypte*, Denon, speaking of a tunic found in a sarcophagus at Thebes and seen by him, tells us that it is " made of a loose fabric of exceedingly fine thread, as thin as that used in the manufacture of lace. It is finer than a hair, twisted and made of two strands, implying either an unheard of skill in hand-spinning, or else machinery of great perfection."

We thus see that the products of the Egyptian workshops were calculated to satisfy the most delicate taste, nor have the artisans of those days ever been surpassed. To convey some idea of the care and watchfulness employed in their production, we must penetrate for a moment into an Egyptian linen manufactory, which we are enabled to do by means of the papyrus, No. 3,930, in the Louvre, interpreted by M. Maspero. This document is nothing but a letter, in which " the scribe *Ah-Mes* complains to the director of the workshop *Taï*, that one of his female hands has been carried off and placed under another employer. He therefore demands her back. But it appears that the removal had been effected at the request of the young workwoman's mother, who charged *Ah-Mes* with keeping her as a simple apprentice, and unfairly profiting by her work, although she was a passed mistress at her trade. *Ah-Mes*, on the other hand, protests of his innocence, declaring that the apprentice is not yet perfect at her work. . . . ." The remainder of the letter is missing.

From this precious little fragment it would appear that every atelier was managed by a head man, under whom were other scribes or masters who looked after a certain number of workmen and especially women ; for, in spite of the testimony of Herodotus, it is certain that women were more especially occupied with this description of handiwork. Each workshop employed a number of apprentices, who received no pay, and the time of whose apprenticeship does not seem to have been clearly settled by law. Hence such cases as that of the document just quoted must have been of frequent occurrence.

Let us now glance at the trade and commercial activity of those remote times, in connection with the subject we are more immediately concerned with.

One cannot but feel astonished at the great industry and flourishing state of all the peoples of Western Asia in those days. Egypt is famous for her embroideries, India for her muslins and dyes, Babylon for her rich tissues, Phœnicia for her purple. All the caravans traversing Persia, Media, and the regions watered by the Indus converge at Babylon, whither also the products of Arabia and Southern India are conveyed by the Arabs and Phœnicians, through the Persian Gulf and the Euphrates. Tyre, also, " the Queen of the Seas," sends her the rich produce of the South, brought by the Egyptian caravans overland, and that of the North by the caravans crossing the Caucasus, Cappadocia, and Asia Minor. It is difficult to suppose that the wealthy Celestial Empire took no part in the great commercial movement; yet China would seem to have long continued in her selfish seclusion, and in spite of all that has been said by the translators of the Bible, Saint Jerome included, silk as an article of trade was still unknown to these trading communities. The Hebrew term *bus*, translated by the word *sericum*, silk, and which has given rise to so much controversy, in the opinion of all Orientalists is nothing but *byssus*, linen, although later on the Romans applied this term to a kind of silk, of a golden yellow hue, peculiar to them.

The Greeks, who borrowed so much from the Egyptians, brought from Egypt the art of manufacturing textile fabrics, as well as the use of paper ($\beta\iota\beta\lambda o\varsigma$), current there nearly two thousand years before the Christian era.

Athens was at an early period a large consumer of textile stuffs, and we know that it was long a great woollen and linen mart. The embellishment of such fabrics was inspired by the works of the great artists of which Greece seemed to be the cradle, and designs of exquisite taste were worked into the materials woven in Athens and the principal cities of the Archipelago. Their warlike expeditions to India, Persia, and especially Media, were attended with important results for the art in question. The purple and gold glistening on the bright coloured dress of the races subdued by the Greeks, excited the avidity of the conquerors, whose attire soon equalled or surpassed in splendour that of the peoples overcome by them.

The Romans, in their turn, inherited something of the culture of the Egyptians, Greeks, and all other nations with whom they came in contact, and from them acquired the art of manufacturing textile goods. They successively adopted the arts and fashions of the Etruscans, Carthagenians, Greeks, Egyptians, and Persians; nor did they spare any pains to equal, if not even to outstrip, their masters. From Phrygia they brought those *plumarii* or artists skilled in embroidering on linen all manner of figures, especially birds, with all the varied hues of their plumage. Gold and silver thread was employed to enhance the brilliancy of such tissues, the exquisite quality of which was universally admired. These workmen were known as *Phrygiones*, from the name of their native country.

Still the Romans themselves were not artists: they knew nothing of the dignity of art, the cultivation of which was comprised by them amongst the servile pursuits, and left to strangers. The free and esteemed artists of Greece were slaves or freedmen in Rome, whence a marked difference in the works of art produced by them.

The question arises whether the Romans invented what may be looked upon as the first germ of true lace-work. The *scutulata vestis*, worn by persons of good position in Rome, was a kind of toga made of a material " whose borders were woven in small network fashion, the netting being all joined together and worked on to the tissue with the needle."

The Roman matrons, besides their own dress, considered it also their duty to make garments for their husbands, children, and slaves, and we know that Augustus usually wore robes wrought by his wife, sister, and daughters.

These primitive customs prevailed for a long time amongst the Romans, and were by them consecrated at the nuptials by an indispensable ceremony, in which the spindle and the distaff were borne before the bride.

Silk was not introduced into Rome till about the close of the first century before our era. The plunder of the rich provinces of Asia at one time rendered silken fabrics so abundant that both men and women adopted them in their dress, a practice which later on, in the sixteenth year of the new era, was denounced by a decree of the Senate, forbidding the men to disgrace themselves by wearing silk attire: " *Ne serica vestis viros fœdaret.*" (Tacitus, Annal. II., Chap. xxxiii.)

The skill of the *Phrygiones* was exerted to the utmost in the preparation of the *togæ pictæ* or *palmatæ*, worn by successful generals on the occasion of their triumphal entry into Rome. These robes were adorned with "palms of gold embroidered or woven into the fabric." The *Phrygiones* also usually manufactured the *trabea*, or purple robe used in dressing up the statues of the gods.

This brief sketch of the art illustrated in the present volume would be incomplete without some reference to the colours employed by the ancients in dyeing their textile fabrics.

The purple, so prized by the Greeks and Romans, and regarded by them as one of the prerogatives of sovereign power, was a sort of deep violet, and not, as is generally supposed, a dye of a bright red colour. Especially famous was the *Porphyra dibapha*, or twice dyed purple, and the practice of thus twice dipping it seems to go back to a very remote period.

This rich colour came from the East, and especially from Phœnicia, and was sold for its weight in silver. Its peculiar value in the eyes of the ancients seems to have been due to the property it possessed of growing more bright and intense by exposure to the sun, instead of fading like most other red, violet, and blue colours.

According to an ancient tradition its discovery was due to chance. We have all heard of the shepherd's dog that, driven by hunger, devoured a certain shell-fish (*Murex*) on the sea-shore, thereby dyeing his mouth with a colour that excited the admiration of all who saw it.

At Pompeii there were found, near the workshop of some dyers, heaps of the shells of the *Murex*, and M. de Saulcy tells us that he came upon similar accumulations in the neighbourhood of Sidon. All these shells bore the marks of the millstone, leaving no doubt that they had been used to extract the dye of the Tyrian purple.

Pliny and Vitruvius speak of the madder plant as one of the ingredients in the purple dye. This may have been a Roman innovation, which must have imparted, if not more brilliancy, at least more durability to the original colour.

The dyeing properties of the pastil (*Isatis*), generally known as woad or dyer's woad, was also known to the ancients. From this plant they extracted a beautiful blue colour; and Pliny tells us that the Roman dyers excelled in its preparation.

We may also mention the Kermes grains, weld or wold, cudbear, indigo, and carmine, all of which were employed in India from time immemorial, and must have been also known to the Romans. Vitruvius tells us that with the juice of many fruits and flowers they were able to produce all sorts of colours, but he has omitted to mention the name or nature of such herbs.

But whatever the means employed, dyeing must necessarily have advanced step by step with the improvements introduced in the manufacture and embellishment of textile fabrics. Thus the embroiderers (*plumarii* or *Phrygiones*) on the one hand, and on the other the dyers (*tinctores*) contributed to the adornment of these materials, and we are accordingly justified in concluding that an art which had flourished in China from the remotest times, which was practised in Egypt fifteen hundred, and in Greece five or six hundred years before our era, did not make shipwreck in Imperial Rome.

Thenceforth nothing has been invented; we have but rediscovered and possibly improved upon the means employed by our predecessors, as we shall endeavour to show in the following chapters.

II.

ETWEEN the ancient society that perishes with the Roman Empire and the modern world that grows out of mediæval times there intervene six centuries of toilsome preparation, during which all the active forces destined to produce a new civilization are at work confusedly and, as it were, in a vast chaos." (DEMOGEOT, *History of French Literature.*)

It would be difficult more vividly to describe the condition to which all the peoples were reduced that formed an integral part of the Roman system and fell with its destruction. Still, the gloomy descriptions that Pope Agatho and other contemporary writers have left us of that period of transition need not be taken too literally, especially in all that concerns the present subject. The invasions of the barbarians, the political and religious troubles, no doubt disturbed, but did not extinguish all artistic life. The fine arts were cultivated not only in Italy, but also in Gaul, even after the Franks had established themselves there. Whatever the issue of battles, whether victory favoured the Cæsars or the barbarians, industry was still necessarily called into requisition, in order to minister to the constant demands of luxury. This truth is confirmed by a passage in the writings of Gregory of Tours, who tell us that even in those unsettled times the pilgrimages to the East redounded to the advancement of the industrious arts. On the evidence of the devout pilgrims returning from the Holy Land, he speaks of *cotton*, which he describes as " a wool which is spun like that of sheep, and of which garments (*indumenta*) are manufactured. Near Jericho there are trees that produce wool (*arbores quæ lanas gignunt*). Their fruit, resembling small gourds, is covered with a somewhat rough skin that serves to protect the down contained in them. I had already heard this produce spoken of, and was at last enabled to see and handle it, not without admiring its extreme whiteness and delicacy (*candorem et subtilitatem earum.*" (GREG. of Tours, *De gloria martyrum.*)

It is curious to find Herodotus a thousand years previously expressing himself much to the same effect when describing the cotton plant, and the passage in the third book of Virgil's " Georgics " bearing on the same point is too well known to be here quoted.

At a very remote epoch the Indians knew how to produce the most varied articles from this plant, which they called *tala*. A Chinese writer, who flourished in the sixth century, refers to the exquisite muslins, embroidered with gold and silver, manufactured in the principal cities of India, and his patriotic spirit takes fire at the sight of the noble daughters of the lettered classes preferring for a moment these foreign materials to the queenly and brilliant silken fabrics of his native land.

The wealth and splendour of the maritime cities of Campania and Calabria, of Venice, and the Tuscan and Lombard commonwealths, arose out of the fall of the Western Empire.

To Gaul the consequences of that event were entirely different, nor did the period of her artistic regeneration set in till much later on.

Still the Roman eagles when withdrawing from that country did not carry with them that taste and love of many-coloured fabrics which distinguished its inhabitants. We know that while the Iberians of Spain wore coarse and dark coloured woollen garments, the Gauls were remarkable for their brilliant dress, at times enriched with precious stones and striped with bright colours. *Virgatis fulgent sagulis*, says Virgil, speaking of the ancient Gaubish military cloaks. This passion for finery required to be constantly ministered to, and the native looms, set up in rivalry of those of Greece and Rome, long resisted the rude shocks of successive inroads, though at last driven to take shelter in the cloister and the church. Hence it is in these hallowed retreats that was mainly fostered the practice of adorning textile fabrics, carried by Christian art to such a high pitch of perfection. Henceforth the monastic foundations not merely opened a new refuge to the scattered remains of science and letters, but also usually grew into centres of industrial life. Handicrafts of all sorts became a clerical pursuit, practised under the shadow of the church by wealthy and powerful associations.

" I doubt not," remarks M. Blanqui, in his history of Political Economy, " that such was the true beginning of the industrial guilds. Their rise is identified with that of the convents where work was prescribed. Hence industry, a slave amongst the Romans, a serf amongst the Franks, came forth free and emancipated to settle in the heart of the mediæval hanse towns."

The bishops and abbots encouraged the manufacture especially of those ornamental fabrics that enhanced the pomp of religious worship. Hence those marvellous copes still jealously preserved in the churches, which astonish us by a finished workmanship, even now all but defying imitation.

The higher clergy set the example by themselves engaging in such occupations. The reliquaries adorned with gold and jewels, made by Saint Eloi, to be placed on the shrines of the saints, were usually covered with a silk veil (*palla holoserica*) mostly woven in the precincts of the cloisters. At that time these veils, always embellished with costly embroidery, were much used in the sacred edifices. Gregory of Tours frequently mentions these admirable fabrics, and in contemporary documents there occur long descriptions of tapestries of diverse sorts hung on the walls of the churches ; some entirely of silk, others enriched with pictorial representations and braided chequer-work.

Those pious and fervent worshippers did but follow the tradition of the primitive Church. Frequent pilgrimages to the Eternal City had made them acquainted with the catacombs, where they also had prayed and admired the first genuine monuments of Christian art—frescoes illustrating scenes from Holy Writ, and in which they discovered the prototypes followed by their predecessors in adorning the sacred fabrics of their churches.

The subterranean church of St. Clement, at Rome, has been recently exposed to view. It contains the oldest and largest mural paintings anywhere to be met with outside the catacombs.

Those touching " ex-votos " still to be seen on the pilastres supporting the vault of the building, that series of frescoes representing the history of its foundation soon after Constantine's great victory, must also have served as models for the skilled embroiderers employed at a great outlay by the religious establishments.

Still such sumptuous display in the House of the Lord was deplored by some austere " servants of the servants of God " (servi servorum Dei), as the Roman pontiffs entitled themselves. Saint Cæsarius also, Bishop of Arles in the sixth century, forbade, especially in nunneries, the use of ornaments embroidered in silk or in bombycine, and hurls fearful anathemas against such stray sheep as did not yield obedience to his injunctions. One may well understand the holy zeal of the venerable prelate, especially in respect of the bombycine, that ephemeral fabric of antiquity. Its extreme delicacy is praised by Tibullus, who describes it as " lighter than the wind, clearer than glass." Pliny is indignant at its being used as a summer garment, doubtless on account of its unseemly transparency, and Juvenal does not fail to aim the shafts of his satire against those effeminate Romans and courtesans who showed a special fondness for this gossamer fabric.

Of what then was it composed ? Whence came it originally ? Were there any just grounds for all the favour shown it on the one hand, and the anger it inspired on the other ? According to Aristotle, it was formed of the silk-like threads obtained by spinning the cocoons of certain worms gathered from the oak and ash of the Attic forests. He also tells us that in the island of Cos, bombycine was first discovered, a fabric which, long mistaken for silk, induced the belief that this precious material had been introduced into Rome from a very remote period.

The garments made of bombycine were known by the expressive terms, nebulæ vestes, vitreæ vestes. But in spite of its diaphanous nature, it fell into disuse with the appearance of silk in the great emporium of Byzantium.

With the fourth century silken fabrics became widely known to the nations of the West. Klaproth, who accompanied the Russian Embassy to China in 1805, and thence brought back many curious records, explains the principal causes of the great impulse given to the silk trade about that time. According to the Chinese legend related by him, a certain king of Khotan, a province at that time independent of China, obtained the emperor's daughter in marriage. The princess, " fairer than a sunbeam, more wayward than the shepherd's star," when departing for her new home could not resist the temptation of violating the laws of the empire, and bringing with her the precious germ to which it owed so much of its wealth and all its lovely costumes. But how effect her purpose ? The happy thought occurred to her of concealing it in her head-dress; for who would dare to lay a rude hand on her fair and waving locks ? And who could suspect those charmingly disposed masses of hair of concealing the priceless treasure ?

Having thus found its way beyond the frontiers of China, silk soon penetrated through Bokhara and Persia to Europe. China herself was fain to follow its westward march, and to export a commodity of which she had so long retained the exclusive monopoly.

The great commercial movement took place about the time that the seat of power was shifted from Rome to Byzantium, and it must have largely contributed to that amazing extravagance and luxury by which the capital of the Lower Empire soon became distinguished. The new generation of Cæsars adopted the pomp of the Eastern Courts, and the gold and silver brocades, the brilliant dyes, the embroidered fabrics of Phœnicia were imitated and soon rivalled in the Imperial workshops.

No question can be raised as to the Indian or Chinese source of the designs adopted in adorning the fabrics manufactured in Constantinople, and against which Chrysostom and so many other venerable prelates raised their warning and indignant voices. Those types of animals or fabulous creatures created by Eastern symbolism and retained by Christian Byzantium, those more or less grotesque figures embellishing the senatorial robes, and spoken of by Ammianus Marcellinus, those exotic flowers, those square, round, and diamond patterns can have had no other origin. The subjects illustrating hunting and fishing, also common in the Eastern Empire, were borrowed from Persian painting and sculpture. Thus Byzantine art was at first imitative, not till long after acquiring a distinct original character.

But, whatever their origin, the authoritative voice of the fathers of the Church was in vain raised against their profuse extravagance. Gold and silver thread, pearls and precious stones, continued to sparkle on the dress of people of distinction. Nothing could arrest the progress of that unbridled luxury which soon received a fresh stimulus from the introduction of sericulture in the Eastern Empire. Procopius relates how, towards the middle of the sixth century, the silkworms' eggs contrived at last to penetrate within the walls of Byzantium. Some Persian monks, after evangelizing certain Indian regions, brought thence a large number of the precious germs, skilfully concealed in their bamboo canes. These they had hatched, and reared the worms according to the method practised in the country whence they had come. Justinian, to whom they revealed the true nature of the little insects, handsomely rewarded the enterprise of the brave missionaries.

Whilst the Eastern Empire brought the art of ornamenting textile fabrics to the highest degree of perfection, the West, though less distinguished, had not remained stationary. Notwithstanding the zeal of the fathers, gorgeous fabrics and the richest tapestries continued to be sold and even manufactured under the very shadow of the churches they were intended to decorate. The decrees of Pope Sylvester and of many local synods passed unheeded, and the wealth of embroidery lavished on the priestly robes knew no bounds.

All these church ornaments, hightened by gold and silver thread, at times by sparkling gems, spread abroad a taste for costly fabrics and tapestries. The art of manufacturing and embellishing them, that had taken refuge in the cloister, found such retreats the more unsuitable in proportion as the great and noble of the land began to have recourse to them. Rich materials were in demand not only for decorating apartments, but also for the tents of kings and feudatory lords, for war, the chase, and the tournament. Nor did the noble dames long remain satisfied with subjects drawn from the Old Testament, but required others also borrowed from the great epic poems of mediæval chivalry, and the pleasant legends of classic times. Such profane commissions were necessarily declined by the stern inmates of the cloisters, and their workshops fell accordingly into disfavour.

From time out of mind there had flourished at the Abbey of Saint Florent de Saumur a manufactury of famous fabrics and tapestries, woven by the monks themselves. Other monastic ateliers existed elsewhere, but their importance everywhere declined in proportion as the secular workshops began to develop, and especially after those of Flanders and Artois were again revived. This worldly competition with the ecclesiastical establishments was strengthened by the trade established by the Moors in Spain.

Certain royal Courts also attracted to themselves the skilled craftsmen whom the cloisters had ceased to employ. More than one great lady condescended to direct the manufacture of the rich materials required for her personal use. We know that Giselle, wife of Saint Stephen, King of Hungary, who flourished about the year one thousand of our era, had induced her royal consort to establish weaving and embroidering ateliers near the Court. The Queen's female embroiderers invented that famous "point de Hongrie," by which expression are still technically known three stripes laid side by side, ladder fashion, used chiefly in embroidering the plumage of birds.

The looms of Artois, that during the sad Merovingian period had almost ceased to produce, were revived and recovered their former renown during the second French dynasty. The products of Artois had already been highly esteemed in Imperial Rome, and though the Romans may have preferred those of the Phrygians, they still had recourse to the woollen stuffs of Gaul, whose reputation had long been universally established.

The stimulus imparted to trade by the first Crusade was destined to give a great expansion to the art here treated of, and it will be seen from the following pages that the French and Italian workshops received therefrom a wide and lasting development.

Britain seems from the earliest times to have possessed native textile products varying both in their materials and designs, and of the same colours as those of the distinctive woollen garments worn by the three traditional Bardic orders.

Later on the Saxons developed a national school of art, the first germs of which would seem to have been brought from the North by the first Scotch, or rather Irish, missionaries, and from the South by the Roman evangelists of the latter end of the sixth and beginning of the seventh century. The devices with which they embellished their manuscripts and jewellery are still remarkable for their extreme richness and ingenuity. When letters and the arts began to revive in the West, mainly through the enterprising and enlightened spirit of the English and Irish missionaries, and under the fostering care of the Teutonic Emperor, Charles the Great, these English artistic works acquired a wide repute on the mainland. Thus we read that Saint Bernward, Bishop of Hildesheim (ca. 960—1022), the greatest patron of the arts in his day, and himself highly skilled in all the formative arts, devoted a careful study to the Irish vases and the works of the English goldsmiths that found their way to the Imperial Frankish Court at Aix-la-Chapelle.

After the Conquest the English looms must have soon become busy again, for Matthew of Westminster, complaining of the ruin of our export trade in woollen stuffs in his time, assures us that with these goods England had formerly supplied the world: " O Anglia olim gloriosa . . . tibi benedixerunt omnium latera nationum de tuis ovium velleribus calefacta."

Woollen cloth weaving was again introduced in 1330, and Bath, Worcester, Norwich, and other places became famous for the produce of their looms. The commoner sorts of silks also, and those of wider breadth, began to be produced in the reign of Edward III., and specimens of these textiles, including some velvets, are contained in the Brooke Collection. But even at an earlier date frequent reference is made to the beauty and wide repute of English needlework.

It would seem that the lighter and more tasteful webs were produced mostly in the nunneries, few of which lacked one of those peculiar horizontal looms we see illustrated in the splendidly illuminated " Bedford Book of Hours," (f. 32), where the Virgin is represented *seated*, weaving curtains for the Temple. The skilful workmanship and elegance in design of these articles may be judged of from several specimens in South Kensington ; amongst others, the fragment, No. 1,256, narrow orphrey web, crimson ground, design in gold ramified scrolls with beasts and birds.

During the fourteenth century, Ailesham, in Lincolnshire, was noted for its fine linen napery, and mention occurs of a towel of this cloth (unum manutergium de Eylisham), owned by the Bishop of Exeter in 1327. It was a time when we had not yet become " a tubbing people."

In the English Benedictine monasteries were produced some coarser fabrics in thread and wool, and a mixture of both, known as " burel."

Abundant contemporary evidence goes to show that many of these textiles were ornamented with highly artistic and tasty devices, and that their fame was by no means limited to these islands. Thus we read, on the one hand, that Sir John Cobham, in 1394, bequeathed to his heirs a bed of Norwich material, embroidered with butterflies (*Testamenta Vetusta*, edited by Nicolas I., 136) ; and on the other, that Charles V. of France prided himself on the possession of an English " hulling," or " halling," as the hangings of those times were called, described as " une salle d'Angleterre vermeille brodée d'azur, et est la bordeure à vignettes et le dedans de lyons, d'aigles, et de lyepars." (MS. No. 8,356, in the Paris National Library, quoted by MICHEL.)

But the Puritans came, and not only destroyed the arts then flourishing, but stamped all artistic feeling out of the heart of the nation. All the formative arts may be said to have ceased for a time to exist, and nothing remained but a continuous, never failing, sparkling stream of poetry to prove that we never ceased to rank amongst the most imaginative peoples in the world.

Under some happy influences, however, the artistic sense began again to reveal itself in ceramics, painting, engraving, and some other branches, and these arts have continued ever since to flourish in England, and to hold their own in honourable rivalry with foreign competitors.

But although the weaving itself of textile fabrics has reached an unsurpassed degree of perfection, the art of ornamenting them can scarcely be said to have ever thoroughly revived the disastrous consequences of Puritanical rule. Yet without such revival our textile industries cannot hope much longer to maintain their supremacy in the foreign market. Hence the paramount duty incumbent on our manufacturers, master weavers, and others interested in the prosperity of the country, to leave nothing undone to develop a genuine artistic taste amongst the people, and especially amongst the intelligent artisans employed by them. To the silk weaver, the carpet manufacturer, the paper maker, and to producers of every description of fancy textile goods, the present work, it is hoped, may prove of special value, as suggesting useful and practical hints to their designers. They will here find suggestions for working drawings in every conceivable style and suitable to all tastes. Should it meet with the encouragement anticipated for it, we propose to follow it up by a second series of a similar nature.

I.

EGYPTIAN ART.

LINEN AND WOOL.

EPOCH OF THE PHARAOHS.

Of all the nations of antiquity the Egyptians were the most skilled and accomplished in the Arts we are here concerned with. They have bequeathed us types and models that we have been able to do no more than imitate.

Our historical sketch has shown how systematically their workshops were conducted, and we have now to examine the results of that organization.

It it difficult to believe that during the French expedition to Egypt there were discovered in the tombs of the Pharaohs fabrics more delicate, more finished, in a word, more perfect than the very best produced in the present day. The collection made of them at the time is one of the wonders to be seen in the Turin Museum. It includes specimens of fine linen, embroideries and ornamental fabrics of various designs, either wrought into the tissue or painted on it. Hence the ancients, like the moderns, employed three distinct decorative processes : *weaving*, *embroidery*, and *painting*.

Our Plate will serve to illustrate these three methods of ornamentation. The sample in the left corner, at the top of the sheet, showing a twining bough with leaves, is a specimen of embroidery in appliqué, copied from the Turin Museum. The blue and white border below it, and from the same collection, seems to have been embroidered with the needle.

The piece following it is one of the finest in the same Museum. It is embellished with bands woven into the fabric, representing the sacred goat and the lotus leaves, symbols of Egyptian worship.

At the foot of the page, and in the left corner, we see a material adorned with rows of scales and a border of diamond pattern. These, with the third sample to the right above, and which is stippled and traced in red and black on a yellow ground, are cloths painted without finish.

All the rest of the Plate, copied in Turin and Naples, is composed of ornamental work on linen, applied after the manner of the painting on the sarcophagi.

England and France are also in possession of some precious specimens of these fabrics. They may be seen at the British Museum, in London, and in the Museums of the Louvre and Saint Germain, in Paris. We have also noticed some interesting samples of the same kind in Marseilles and Lyons.

II.

CHINESE ART.

VARIOUS EPOCHS.

WHEN we consider that the Chinese are our precursors and masters in the art of weaving, we might be led to suppose that amongst them are to be found the oldest and most numerous specimens of it. But this is far from being the case, and nothing is rarer than to meet with specimens of Eastern fabrics of a remote age. This is to be attributed to the exclusive spirit of the Chinese at all epochs, allowing but few of their products to find their way abroad, and these stray samples could scarcely hope to escape the ravages of time.

None of the public or private European collections contain, as far as we know, any very ancient samples of Japanese or Chinese fabrics. Hence the only documents that can be consulted to form an estimate of their art in ornamenting textile fabrics, are their ancient manuscripts and paintings. These show us all sorts of ornamental fabrics, the minutest details of the robes of the mandarins being represented even in their old porcelain. Hence it becomes· easy to supply the gap here alluded to, since, as far as we can go back, we find the same motives employed as at present. These are consequently the faithful copy of those formerly in use.

Our Plate embraces a collection of various specimens, in which we have endeavoured to convey an idea of the taste prevailing at different periods.

The material on a grey ground, above, to the left, and that on a black ground, in the centre, are the oldest types, at first imitated in Persia and Asia, afterwards in Europe.

The two samples at the foot of the page, of floral design and vermiculated, were produced in the fifteenth century.

The right corner, above, shows us some motives imitated by the French manufactories in the seventeenth century. Lastly, the two specimens, right and left of the centre piece, are of more recent date, and betray the influence of European taste.

Ch. Kreutzberger del. Régamey lith.   Imp. Lemercier & Cie. rue de Seine 57 Paris

III.

ARABIC ART.

VARIOUS EPOCHS.

COTTON, LINEN, AND SILKEN FABRICS.

It would be out of place to enter here into a deep study of the strictly Arabic art of decorating textile fabrics. This people drew from all Eastern countries and from all ages the greater part of the motives in decorative work transmitted by them to other nations, either through their settlements in Sicily and Spain, or through the emporiums of Asia and Constantinople.

In our Plate we give a general view of the main sources to which the Arabs had recourse, without however overlooking what may seem to have been peculiar to the Arabic nation itself.

Egypt is undoubtedly the source of the five pieces woven of cotton, of which the first two, in the right and left corners above, show superimposed triangular and red diamond patterns on white ground respectively. The same disposition is again seen in the three smaller motives, right and left of the piece of silk woven with gold Arabic writing.

The sample above it, gold, red and blue, on a white ground, shaded in grey, as well as the specimen beneath in blue, yellow and green, are genuine Arabic designs.

The much more recent influence of Persia or Constantinople is evident in the two remaining subjects, composed of palms and rose work.

3

ART ARABE

Ch Kreutzberger del _ Régamey lith

Imp Lemercier & Cie rue de Seine 57 Paris

IV.

PERSIAN ART.

VARIOUS TYPES.

THE conservative feeling of the Eastern peoples in respect of Art and their profound veneration for tradition prevent us from assigning a fixed date to the manifold products of their looms. The landmarks elsewhere relied on by the archæologist in his investigations here fail him utterly, compelling him to observe great precaution in his conclusions. Still, we may venture to say that the design on a green ground, in the centre of our Plate, may be classed with the numerous specimens representing animals affrontés, that is, facing the spectator, and copied in the Italian looms so early as the thirteenth century.

The palms in the two compositions at the top of the page have been reproduced in all ages; nor can it fail to be interesting to estimate the various Oriental types that have been most frequently imitated in Europe. The material of the design in gold on red ground, and woven of silk, was used for a rich costume. The other, with colours in weft and worked in gold wire, is now used to cover a Venetian statute book, dated 1400.

Of the two other motives at the foot of the sheet, the first, on a brown ground with red graining and yellow twining branches, is the model of numerous fabrics copied in Venice and France at the beginning of the seventeenth century. The second, on blue ground, with "cartouches" set off in gold, and twining branches also in gold, has been and still is constantly imitated by our manufacturers of carpets in the Eastern taste.

4

PERSAN

Ch. Kreutzberger del _ Régamey lith

Imp. Lemercier & Cie rue de Seine 57 Paris

V.

P E R S I A N   A R T.

STRIPED PATTERNS IN SILKS.

STRAIGHT and serpentine lines were introduced at an early date into Persian decorative art, and still form one of its favourite features. Hence if we here assign them to the sixteenth century, we do so rather to indicate the time when they became more generally used than to restrict them to any definite period. They took the place of the animals affrontés, which during the fourteenth and fifteenth centuries were largely copied in the West. It may be added that some old inventories speak of the *Panni virgati*, or striped cloths, but mention is made of them much less frequently than of the " histories of animals."

The square piece in the centre of our Plate, a silk and silver fabric, older than those accompanying it, was found at Siena, in Tuscany, and seems to have served to decorate some church object.

The other fabric, enclosing it like a frame and serving it as a ground, with red and blue waving lines, adorned with gold ornamental work, may also be referred to the sixteenth century.

The four remaining specimens, at top and bottom of the page, were copied at the Historical Exhibition of Costumes, opened at the Palace of Industry, 1874. They present varieties of striped patterns of various epochs; the two lower ones being obviously much older than the others.

PERSAN

Ch Kreutzberger del _ Régamey lith.

Imp Lemercier & Cie rue de Seine 57

VI.

FROM THE EIGHTH TO THE ELEVENTH CENTURY.

SILKS.

CARLOVINGIAN EPOCH.

A RETURN to such a remote past, especially in the matter of textile fabrics, seems now no longer possible without a careful study of the delicate miniatures embellishing the few manuscripts that survive from that time. We must, moreover, rest satisfied with an approximate knowledge of the designs thus revealed to us, and give up all hope of ascertaining anything about the processes employed in their manufacture.

Having been fortunate enough to have met with two specimens of these extremely rare and ancient fabrics, we have spared no pains to reproduce them in a manner worthy of their importance.

While respecting the handiwork of the weaver, years have made sad havoc of its colours. Hence we have endeavoured to make our designs follow a course opposed to that of time, and in spite of the difficulties attending the chromo-lithographic process in representing graduated tones, we have succeeded in giving, on the left of the Plate, the present state of these models, by insensible shadings causing them gradually to survive, and at last reappear to the extreme right in all their pristine splendour.

These specimens belong to the class of mixed materials, woven and twilled in the Eastern manner. Their warp is of coarse linen thread—almost a fine cord or twist—suspended vertically, as is practised in the high warp loom. The weft silk is interwoven with gold threads in the upper, and with silver in the lower sample. These were doubtless fabrics produced from the French looms of the period, and manufactured probably in the precincts of the episcopal residences for the service of the Church.

Ch Kreutzberger del   Régamey lith

Imp Lemercier & Cie rue de Seine 57 Paris

VII.

THIRTEENTH CENTURY.

TYPES OF BIRDS AFFRONTÉ AND PASSANT.

ALTHOUGH of totally distinct kinds, we have reproduced these two pieces on the same Plate, on account of certain points of resemblance in their manufacture, and because they belong to the same epoch, both dating from the second half of the thirteenth century.

The first is in the Cluny Museum, where it is shown, for no apparent reason, in the *Salle des Couronnes d'or*, on the first floor. It is a figured satin, which a slight study will show to be entirely distinct from the Italian fabrics of this class. It seems heavy, lacking that lightness which is the essential property of materials copied on Eastern models. Its texture having more body and fulness owing to the thickness of the silk, produces the effect of real velvet. We believe it to be the product of some loom in the North of Europe. The material of which it is composed, and whose antiquity cannot be gainsaid, seems to be nothing else than "Samite," the generic name of this description of fabric in the Middle Ages.

The second piece, enriched with gold, and the oldest specimen of the kind known to us, belongs to the distinctive *velvet* class, a material even at that remote period largely manufactured.

Ch Kreutzberger del   Régamey lith   Imp Lemercier & Cie rue de Seine 57 Paris

VIII.

THIRTEENTH CENTURY.

SILKS.

PATTERNS WITH FIGURES OF ANGELS.

THE figures of angels, forming the general type of this Plate, are frequently met in the ornamental compositions of the thirteenth century. We have ourselves seen them introduced into a painting on a panel before the altar of one of the chapels in the apsis of the Church of *Santo Spirito*, at Florence. Such figures were also employed by the Limoges enamellers on their reliquaries. Statuaries also carved them on stone, disposing them in diverse ways; and they came at last to be adopted in the ornamentation of textile fabrics.

The first of our specimens, above, to the left, is a Sicilian damask, interwoven with gold, probably of the class formerly known by the name of "Cendal."

The second, occupying the lower part of the Plate, has been copied in the Kensington Museum, and seems to belong to the same country, epoch, and category as the previous. The angels are here disposed in three rows and various attitudes. In the first row the figures face to the left, one of the hands swinging a censer; in the second they are reversed, both hands hold a crown of thorns. The third, here omitted, is a repetition of the first, the only difference being that a cross held erect takes the place of the censer.

Our third design—white on blue ground—belongs to the close of the same century, and is also in South Kensington, where it is catalogued as of Italian origin, an opinion we cannot share in, believing it to be rather the produce of some Northern loom.

Ch. Kreutzberger del. Régamey lith

Imp. Lemercier & Cie rue de Seine 57 Paris

IX.

THIRTEENTH CENTURY.

SILKS.

TYPES WITH ORNAMENTAL HORIZONTAL STRIPES.

We do not fancy that any attempt has yet been made in connection with our subject to separate according to their *types*, and systematically classify the artistic inheritance bequeathed to us by the nations of the East. Yet each of them was variously inspired, and thus acquired a distinct original character by the influence of climate, the animal and vegetable kingdoms familiar to their eyes, and, above all, by the religion professed by them.

A little observation renders it an easy matter to recognise the creations peculiar to these different races, whether jealously retaining their traditions, and condemning themselves, like the Chinese, to absolute immobility, or allowing their posterity to go and widely disseminate abroad the fruitful germ of transmitted ideas, as was the case with the Persians and other peoples of Western Asia.

In the fabrics of our Plate we again meet with the same ornamental elements that appear on the monuments and in the ancient manuscripts of Persia, a resemblance that has already been anticipated in one of our earlier Plates.

The horizontal stripes form a special class of their own, and we here reproduce two fine examples of this sort: the first from the Cluny Museum, from South Kensington, and the Gay Collection in Paris; the second is borrowed from our own private collection.

These fabrics seem to be of Sicilian make, after genuine Persian models. We shall presently meet with another type, which, with the help of the learned M. Lenormand, will enable us to enlarge on this subject.

Ch. Kreutzberger del _ Régamey lith   Imp. Lemercier & Cie rue de Seine 57 Paris

X.

THIRTEENTH CENTURY.

LION PATTERNS.

Of all the members of the animal kingdom, the lion was undoubtedly one of the first employed in the decoration of textile fabrics. Indigenous in the countries where the most costly materials were produced, the fear that he inspired, and the symbol of strength ever associated with his image, rendered him at an early date a fitting subject wherewith to adorn the robes of the great and powerful. Thus he became the emblem of the tribe of Judah, that was to hold the sceptre till the coming of the Messiah, an idea which Champollion found of great help in his first tentative essays at interpreting the hieroglyphics of Egypt.

Our Plate presents us with three magnificent specimens of such symbolical lions. In the first, to the left, the original of which is in our possession, we see, on a red ground interwoven with gold, lions couched at the foot of palm trees, disposed in horizontal lines, alternating with lines of birds representing geese—*union of foresight with strength.*

In the second specimen, also of silk and gold on a red ground, and in the South Kensington Museum, we see lions similarly grouped with eagles—*symbol of power and strength.*

In the third, at the foot of the Plate, in which the silken fabric is of stouter texture, and also interwoven with gold, lions are grouped with doves—*emblem of strength and gentleness.* This specimen is also our property.

After glancing at this threefold embodiment of the same thought, we can scarcely suppose that the artist merely allowed his fancy to yield to a passing inspiration, but rather that his object was to associate its symbolic meaning with the persons for whom such costly stuffs were intended.

We would assign all three samples to the same date (fourteenth century), referring the creation of the type itself to a much more remote period.

XIIIᵉ SIÈCLE

XI.

FOURTEENTH CENTURY.

ASTER PATTERNS.

The name alone of this type would be enough to determine its Eastern origin. The aster was looked on as a sacred plant by the followers of Zoroaster, and so named on account of the resemblance it bore to the stars worshipped by them.

As a typical ornament for tapestries and dress, it came into use towards the close of the thirteenth century, and held its ground throughout the fourteenth and the beginning of the fifteenth. Specimens of these various dates are here reproduced.

That in the centre, to the left, is the oldest. It is a velvet on red ground, set off with green, and interwoven with gold and silver. This fine sample was copied by M. Regamey, from the cover of a manuscript in the National Library at Paris.

The specimen on red satin ground, interwoven in green, with asters of red velvet, is in our own collection. It at once attracts us by its elegant design.

The large piece at top of the sheet is a white velvet, set off with green and red, for which we are indebted to M. Escosura. A similar design is mentioned by M. Paul Lacroix, as employed in the costumes of the fifteenth century. He reproduces it from the taroc-cards invented by J. Gringoneur, for the diversion of King Charles VI.

The subject at the foot of the page, on red ground interwoven with gold, is in our collection. It seems more recent than the others, and may be referred to the beginning of the fourteenth century. It is extremely rich, and conveys a high idea of the luxury of the times.

XII

FOURTEENTH CENTURY.

SILKS.

PATTERNS OF ANIMALS, BIRDS, AND FOLIAGE.

THE four pieces here reproduced from South Kensington are there described as damasks, of Italian workmanship, and referred to the fourteenth century. They would seem to have been produced in Lucca, after Sicilian designs, the Lucca craftsman having come originally from Sicily.

They so closely resemble each other that we may be dispensed from any detailed description of them. They are all on a uniform red ground, interwoven in silk and gold.

XIII.

FOURTEENTH AND FIFTEENTH CENTURIES.

SILKS.

MANY-COLOURED VELVETS.

THESE specimens of polychrome velvets are here grouped together in order the better to illustrate the various kinds of designs adopted during a portion of the fourteenth and throughout the fifteenth century in embellishing this particular material.

Warps and wefts of various colours had long been used in manufacturing velvet, as shown by the splendid specimen we have elsewhere copied from the Fortuny Collection; parrots affrontés alternating with Gothic leaves. Next to it must be placed the velvet, interwoven with gold and decorated with emblems of chivalry, at the top of our Plate, which may be older than the fifteenth century. The helmet decked with plume of feathers was worn so early as the thirteenth century, and according to Mezeray was brought from the East by the Crusaders. On the other hand, the painter Paolo Ucello (1396—1479), in his picture of the Battle of St. Egidio, preserved in the British Museum, shows us the same helmets surmounted by the plume.

There also may be seen a knight's head-dress of a gold velvet with Gothic leaves, in a design similar to that of the centre piece to the left on our Plate. The piece adjoining it, on the right, developed from an oblong curve or "mullion," composed of a wreath of small pomegranates encircling a larger one, belongs to the second half of the fifteenth century, as do also the two subjects at the bottom of the page. That to the left is from the rich Bazilewski Collection, and for the other we are indebted to M. Dreyfus.

XIV.

GOTHIC ART.

FIFTEENTH CENTURY.

MULLION PATTERNS.

WE have borrowed from architecture the technical name of this class of designs, composed of vertical waving lines meeting and diverging at regular intervals, and thus describing a figure strikingly analogous to certain sinuous mullions often employed by the architect and the glass painter in decorating the windows of Gothic buildings.

This style was much in vogue during the fourteenth, the fifteenth, and even the beginning of the sixteenth century. It may be traced in the costumes of persons of distinction, painted by the master enamellers of Limoges, on the tapestries of various Flemish looms, and in the works of the first unknown masters of the Siena and Florentine schools. We may therefore conclude that it is of Eastern origin, going back to a much more remote epoch.

Our Plate comprises four velvet samples. The first, to the left, above, is interwoven with gold, relieved with green on a red ground. Both it and its neighbour to the right —golden yellow on green ground—are in South Kensington; each of them characterized by the aster, which had become the complement of the mullion.

The two other specimens—green on green ground, and green ground with white design—are in our own collection, and show more distinctly the waving lines forming the mullion pattern.

XV.

FIFTEENTH CENTURY.

LOBED GOTHIC LEAF PATTERNS.

WE are unable to state with certainty what is the primitive type either of the lobed Gothic leaf that is detached from its peduncle, as in this Plate; or of the same leaf with its stem, as shown in our next Illustration.

Though seemingly differing little from each other, the decorative effect of these two patterns presents such striking contrasts that they deserve to be separately classified.

The detached leaf seems to claim priority in point of time; its presence being evident in works older than the fifteenth century, towards the close of which the other first makes its appearance. Still, the lobed leaf is employed by Raphael, as in the portrait of Angelo Doni, in the Pitti Gallery, Florence, and on the baldachino, painted on the left of the Battle of Constantine, in the Vatican. This brings us down to the first half of the sixteenth century, so that this type ranges altogether from the fourteenth to the middle of the sixteenth.

The eight velvet and damask specimens on our Plate we have referred to the common date of the fifteenth century. The two centre pieces (one on red ground, in our possession; the other on blue, in South Kensington); the top centre piece, also in South Kensington, and a fourth, in the same place, at the bottom of the page, are all velvets interwoven with gold, and of the pomegranate design.

The specimen in the left corner, above, is a blue damask; that in the right corner, below, a violet damask. The corresponding diagonal shows, in the right corner, above, a plain velvet with yellow design; and in the left, below, a green velvet on green ground. These four corner pieces are all in our collection.

Ch Kreutzberger del _ Régamey lith.

Imp. Lemercier, & Cⁱᵉ rue de Seine 57 Paris

XVI.

FIFTEENTH CENTURY.

ITALIAN TYPES, AFTER EASTERN PATTERNS.

THE weaver's art had already reached such a degree of perfection in the fifteenth century in Italy, that much further improvement was scarcely henceforth to be looked for. The principal towns in the North rivalled each other in the manufacture of velvet, and pure or mixed silks, fabrics both plain and with coloured warp and woof, besides all manner of fancy tissues, requiring the use of several shuttles in their production. Yet notwithstanding all this industry and mutual rivalry, a great indifference continued to be displayed in the matter of decoration, all copying blindly from Eastern models, without ever dreaming of emancipating themselves from such thraldom, or creating new and characteristically national designs.

Here we give four different types of those copies, apparently executed in Venice during the fifteenth century. The two above belong to the pattern of trailing vines, of which our Plates show several other examples. Of the two others, the large one to the right is based on the pomegranate model; and the smaller, to the left, is an adaptation of the mullion. All four are in our own collection.

Ch Kreutzberger del   Régamey lith   Imp Lemercier & Cⁱᵉ rue de Seine 57 Paris

XVII.

SIXTEENTH CENTURY.

SILKS.

PATTERNS OF POMEGRANATE DISPOSED IN CIRCLES.

THE pomegranate enclosed in several circles of flowrets, themselves inscribed within a lobed circle, and serving as connecting links with a final row completing the design, is an Italian creation based on the Gothic lobed leaf, and marking the period of transition from the old Arabic to the more modern European taste. As it thus introduces a new era in the history of our art, it is important carefully to fix the date of its first appearance. It was in general use between 1500 and 1550, which enables us to assign it to the sixteenth century, though casually met with between 1450 and 1500. Hence its creation may be referred to the last years of the fifteenth century. It is introduced by Raphael in his decorations of the Vatican apartments, where we see it in company with the lobed Gothic leaf. We therefore conclude that not till this epoch did Italy produce works of this sort of a truly national character.

The comprehensive nature of the design, its breadth of composition, and the necessity of giving it full effect, have prevented us from reproducing more than two examples of this type. We have, however, chosen them from amongst the finest extant. The upper one is a damask, interwoven with silver of unsurpassed richness; that below it is a velvet, on full figured gold ground. This fine specimen belonged to the Fortuny Collection, of which we have already had occasion to speak.

Ch. Kreutzberger, del.   Régamey, Lith.   Imp. Bachelin-Deflorenne, 13, rue Cassette, Paris.

XVIII.

SIXTEENTH CENTURY.

SPAIN.

SILKS OF VARIOUS CIRCULAR DESIGNS.

THE old reputation acquired by the cities of Almeria, Granada, and Malaga, during the occupation of the country by the Moors, might have secured for Spain a more conspicuous place in our collection, had not the expulsion of the Arabs left the field open to the destructive competition of neighbouring industries. The Italians improved the occasion to such an extent that little was left for the native looms, except to copy the processes and designs of their rivals. This, however, they did to such perfection that it is often difficult, and at times even impossible, to decide whether certain fabrics are the produce of Italian or Spanish looms. From all this it follows that there are very few types peculiar to Spain, and that the textile fabrics of this country are easily confounded with those of its neighbours.

The first two specimens, in the upper part of our Plate, belong to those patterns characterized by the figure of a perfect circle, and recall the Moorish designs of the thirteenth and fourteenth centuries, modified by the taste of the Renaissance.

The red sample, below, shows us an oval form, implying a tendency towards Italian designs. They are all three of silk damask, which was used in the manufacture of sacerdotal robes.

Ch. Kreutzberger, del.   Régamey, Lith.   Imp. Bachelin-Deflorenne, 13, rue Cassette, Paris.

XIX.

SIXTEENTH CENTURY.

SILKS.

DOUBLE MULLION FUNICULAR PATTERN.

THIS pattern is characterized by a double mullion encircling the pomegranate, as well as by the looped cord on the larger of the two enclosures, and dividing it into several sections. It is of Italian origin, and was evidently developed out of the simple mullion. It may be referred to the opening of the sixteenth century, and frequently occurs on works coincident with the declining years of Raphael. All the glass painters of the sixteenth century introduced it into the costumes of their figures, and it was employed in the ornamentation of all sorts of fabrics—velvets, damasks, imitation brocades—showing that it was in no less favour with the general public than with the professional artists of the period.

The grey sample, in the right upper corner of our Plate, is a silk damask, the crown figuring in it connecting it chronologically with the simple crowned mullion pattern. Its neighbour, on the left—yellow imitation brocade—calls for the same remark, in respect of the large floral ornament attached to the mullion, and forming a connecting link between this type and the other just spoken of.

The two lower specimens—one velvet on yellow satin ground, set off with bright lilac; the other imitation brocade, with red design on yellow ground—are the finest patterns and the most perfect embodiment of the double mullion.

Ch. Kreutzberger, del.   Régamey, Lith   Imp. Bachelin Deflorenne, 13, rue Cassette, Paris.

XX.

SIXTEENTH CENTURY.

VELVETS.

POMEGRANATE PATTERNS.

WE consider it a duty to retain as far as possible the typical names already consecrated by established usage. The Nürnberg and South Kensington Museums in their descriptive catalogues employ indifferently the general term pomegranate to denote this ornamental feature, whether fruit or flower, occupying the centre of designs of this sort, although as often resembling the thistle flower as the fruit in question.

While, therefore, still adopting this distinctive term, we shall restrict it to such undecided specimens as may not require a more definite name. Thus, in our Plate, the medallion enclosing the pomegranate presents no features sufficiently distinct to form a general type. This design can therefore be distinguished by the central flower alone.

These velvets seem to have been manufactured in Florence during the Medicean epoch. We know that the workshops of that city were placed under the direct patronage of the Medici, who took a great interest in them, and were ever jealous of their rivalry over all other competitors.

The largest specimen was found in Florence ; the others have been copied in Bologna and other Italian towns.

Ch. Kreutzberger del _ Régamey lith

Imp. Lemercier & Cⁱᵉ rue de Seine 57 Paris

XXI.

SIXTEENTH CENTURY.

SILKS AND VELVETS.

BUCKLE AND LOOPED PATTERNS.

THE adoption of the buckle towards the end of the fifteenth and beginning of the sixteenth century enriched our art with a new motive destined to heighten its effects. It seems to have been originally adopted from the province of embroidery, where we have frequently met with it always in very happy combinations. It adapted itself so readily to velvet materials at a time when their manufacture had reached such perfection, that the idea once suggested was forthwith realized.

This costly process, consisting in covering the fabric with metal in relief, in form of a number of little buckles closely linked together, is one of the most sumptuous motives available in the ornamentation of textile fabrics. It would be difficult to judge of its effect in the examples here given, did we not add that in the two central specimens the looping is indicated by the yellow stipplings on gold ground, so that of the velvet there remains nothing but the red tracing of the design, while in the lower one it is marked by the transverse lines of the ground itself.

On the left, the gold stippling on red ground represents the loops, while to the right some silver portions are executed in loops of this metal.

But few examples of such costly materials have survived; besides the specimens in our own collection, the only amateurs known to us who possess any similar ones are Baron Rothschild, M. Basilewski, and Prince Demidoff, who purchased the church ornaments of the Fortuny Collection.

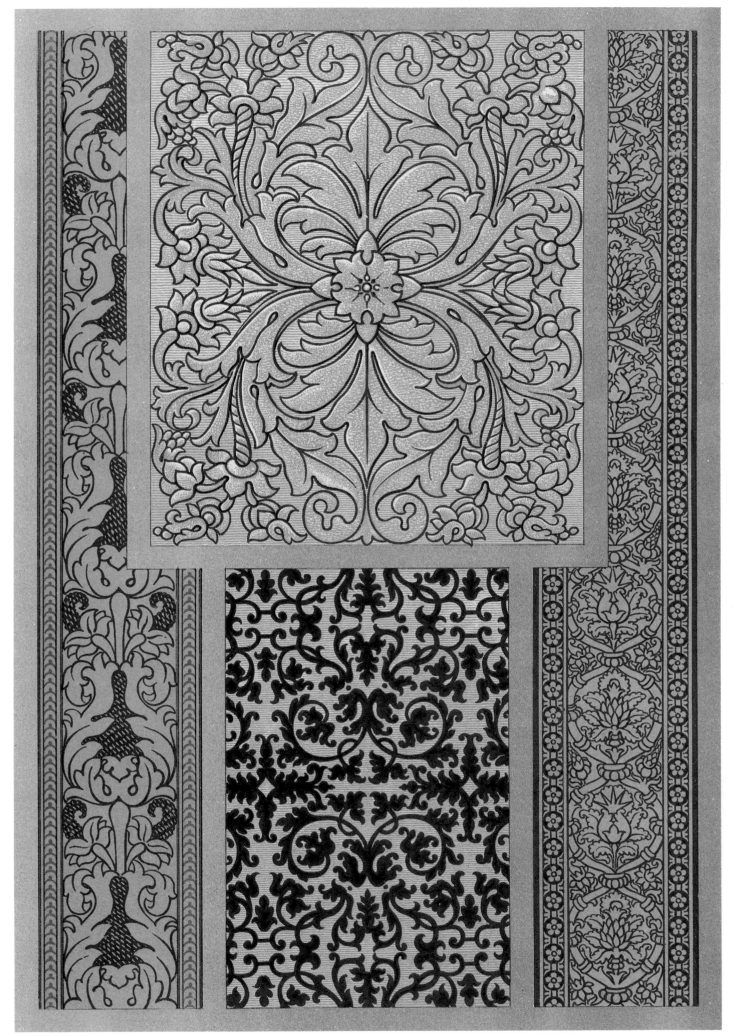

Ch. Kreutzberger, del.   Régamey, Lith.   Imp. Bachelin-Deflorenne, 13, rue Cassette, Paris

XXII.

SIXTEENTH CENTURY.

SILKS.

RETICULATED MULLION PATTERNS.

In order the better to realize the nicer differences in the class of designs to which we have given the generic name of *mullions*, we must invite particular attention to the variety known as *foliated mullions*, represented by the specimen in the upper left corner of our Plate. It is all the more necessary to attend to this point, because the red damask interwoven with gold of this design is connected by its sinuous elliptical form with the *foliated crowned mullions*, to which one of our Plates is exclusively devoted, while still differing essentially from them in its large floral details, connecting it more with the design here under consideration.

This remark will at the same time suffice to show that both types must be referred to the same epoch. Thus in the three other examples reproduced on our Plate we observe the delicate and elegant curvilinear design replaced by lines of straighter form connecting them with diamond and square types, and justifying their being classed apart.

A sample of the first specimen belongs to the Lyons Museum, and is referred to the year 1500. The other three are also faithfully reproduced from originals of 1540 or earlier.

Ch Kreutzberger del _ Régamey lith

Imp Lemercier & C.ᵉ rue de Seine 57 Paris

XXIII.

SIXTEENTH CENTURY.

SPANISH RAISED EMBROIDERIES.

TWINING FOLIAGE PATTERNS.

ALL Europe had been converted to the worship of the Renaissance, when Francis I., in the first half of the sixteenth century, attracted the Florentine and Bolognese artists to his Court. Charles V. had shown himself no less anxious than his rival to have his palaces in Madrid and Germany decorated in this new style, while Henry VIII. had, in 1520, picked up the gauntlet in the rivalry of pomp and display, that has given to the famous tristing place of the sovereigns of France and England the name of the "Field of the Cloth of Gold."

A reminiscence of these historic pages has been preserved by Holbein in a series of paintings now in Hampton Court. In one of them we see Henry VIII. seated on a low throne, dressed in a costume of red velvet embroidered in gold. At his feet is a cushion embroidered in the same metal, and in Renaissance designs. In another of the compositions, representing the *Interview between the Kings of England and France*, may be seen the designs of the gold embroideries decorating the tents of the rival camps— also illustrating the new taste of the close of the fifteenth century.

In our Plate may be seen further illustrations of the embroiderer's art during the sixteenth century. In previous examples we were able to notice the means employed to fill in rectangles horizontally or longitudinally disposed. In order as far as possible to meet the requirements of the trade we here give the composition of square surfaces.

Ch. Kreutzberger, del.   Regamey, Lith.

Imp Rachelin-Deflorenne, 13, rue Cassette, Paris

XXIV.

SIXTEENTH CENTURY.

VELVETS.

FLORAL PATTERNS.

FLOWER WORK, which in the previous types held but a subordinate place in the general design, became towards the middle of the sixteenth century the exclusive motive of the composition. The lobed Gothic leaf of the fifteenth, as well as the floral circles of the close of that period, were entirely set aside. The floral design was now placed at the point of intersection of lines traced in counter-simple, where it always produced a fine effect.

Our two specimens are very remarkable, especially the first for the variety of its hues, showing that at this time the tradition had not yet been forgotten of those many-coloured velvets of the fifteenth century, to which two of our Plates have been set apart. Here also we may call attention to the delicacy and lightness of the tones, which, in spite of their sharp contrasts and quaint disposition, still unite in bringing about an agreeable and harmonious general effect.

The second, with green designs on white ground, and of the same description as the foregoing, is scarcely less interesting. The design is surmounted by the pomegranate reduced in size, but presenting absolutely the same description as in the more intricate compositions illustrated farther back. By retracing in thought the five or six lobes of the Gothic leaf that encircled it, we may restore the design of a velvet of the fifteenth century. Here also the harmony is perfect, the usual law of the blending of colours being strictly followed.

Ch Kreutzberger del . Régamey lith

Imp Lemercier & Cie rue de Seine 57 Paris

XXV.

SIXTEENTH CENTURY.

COMPOSITE PATTERNS.

NEW APPLICATION OF ANIMALS AFFRONTÉS.

In the sixteenth century a radical change was effected by Raphael in the art of designing. The stiff and conventual forms of his predecessors he replaced by the truth and simplicity of models after nature, thus giving a fresh impulse to every branch of the industrial arts, and more especially to that of the weaver, who now cast about for new motives while receiving fresh inspiration from the older stock subjects.

This is well seen in the two longitudinal samples, right and left of our Plate. Here we have birds, lions, stags, and leopards, addorsed or affontés; now at rest on the serpentine lines of the mullions, as in that to the right; now on the different sectional designs, as in that to the left.

In the middle of the sheet we have placed a very fine damask, copied under our eyes in the Colonna Palace, by Signor Marchetti, a gifted Roman artist, to whom we are indebted for some magnificent transcripts of the sort. This crowned and branching mullion design shows in the centre the figure of a Mélusine with a fish's tail (a common motive towards the end of the sixteenth century), surmounted by the Colonna arms. Hence we have here a design evidently made to order, a circumstance not lacking in interest.

Below this is a red and brown silk of the crowned mullion pattern, adopting a vase for the motive of its interior. The green and white specimen in the left corner, above, is from a chimneypiece in the Colonna Palace, and the other pieces form part of our collection. They all belong to the middle of this century, and we have noticed similar ones in the paintings of Tintoret (1512–1594), at Genoa.

Ch. Kreutzberger del _ Régamey lith

Imp. Lemercier & Cie rue de Seine 57 Paris

XXVI.

SIXTEENTH CENTURY.

APPLIQUÉ EMBROIDERY.

SPANISH PATTERNS.

EMBROIDERY, owing to the greater freedom of its rules and its richer effects, adopted more readily than weaving the motives of Arabic architecture, and in Spain assumed a special Oriental character peculiar to that country. It is not a little remarkable that artistic germs when transported to foreign soil usually produce works characteristic of the genius of both nationalities, thus resulting in a new and distinctive style.

In the two specimens at top of our Plate we cannot fail to recognise the Moorish type, blended with the ordinary motives of the Renaissance.

Below them are five pieces, illustrating in the Spanish manner some of the types already classified by us. On the left we have reticulated work, embellished with a vase and flowers; on the right, a crowned mullion, filled in with a fruit of a peculiar round shape, and surmounted by a fancy crown; in the centre, a motive arranged in sections, alternating with mullions in the Italian Renaissance taste; below, on the left, a frieze with the reversed F pattern; on the right, the design of a vase strewn with flowers.

To M. Lévy we are indebted for the first sample in the right corner, above, and the last in the left corner, below.

ESPAGNE
XVIᴱ SIÈCLE

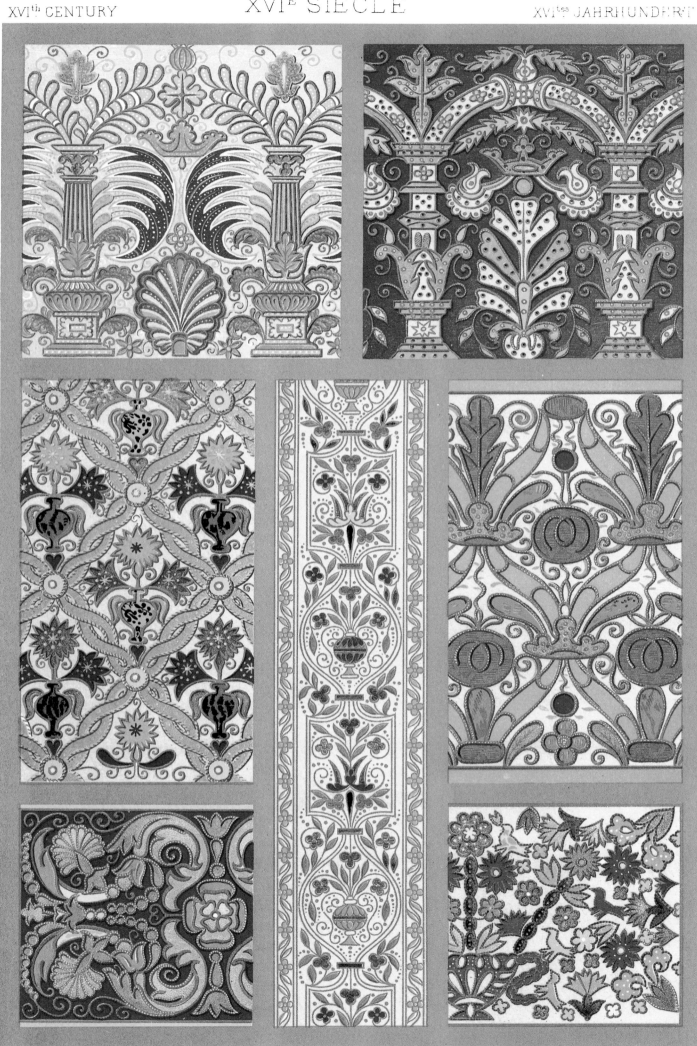

Ch. Kreutzberger, del.   Régamey, Lith.   Imp. Bachelin-Deflorenne, 13, rue Cassette, Paris

XXVII.

SIXTEENTH CENTURY.

EMBROIDERIES.

RENAISSANCE BED HANGINGS.

ACCORDING to the old chroniclers, whenever the Court was removed or the King had to undertake a journey, it became necessary not only to provide suitable accommodation for him in the castle or neighbouring abbey, but also to take care that he was becomingly entertained without involving his host in ruinous expenses. Hence he was on such occasions preceded by the royal messengers sent on to prepare the apartments he was to occupy.

On this custom Charles of Orleans has left us some curious details in a charming little rondeau, here subjoined:

> Les fourriers d'este sont venuz
> Pour appareiller son logis,
> Et ont fait tendre ses tappis
> De fleurs et verdure tissuz.
> En estendant tappis veluz
> De vert herbe par le pais,
> Les fourriers d'este sont venuz.

To some such circumstance we are indebted for the two panels, here reproduced, of the most sumptuous bed cornice left us by the Renaissance. It is composed of thirteen pieces, all of different designs, on diapered velvet ground, with silk interwoven in silver, in appliqué, and heightened with colours, fine pearls and garnets.

This rich piece of embroidery, according to the tradition, was given by Henry II. to the convent of La Trappe, near Montagne, on the occasion of a short stay made in it by him on his way to Brittany.

In order to preserve in its purity the photographic transcription of these panels, we have accompanied them with two specimens of gimp (passementerie), in gold and silver, of the same epoch.

Ch Kreutzberger del   Régamey lith   Imp. Lemercier & Cⁱᵉ rue de Seine 57 Paris

XXVIII.

SIXTEENTH CENTURY.

VELVETS.

LOPPED BOUGH PATTERNS.

The type of this design, already in vogue during the previous centuries, occurs on the tokens of recognition distributed amongst the Burgundy party, to distinguish them from the Armagnacs in the famous feud between the houses of Orleans and Burgundy.

The velvets of our Plate, all on a ground worked with gold thread, come from the famous Venetian looms, the superiority of which we shall have more than one occasion to speak of during the sixteenth and seventeenth centuries.

The reputation of these fabrics, whose richness seems never to have been surpassed, was spread throughout Europe. Adopted for doublets and gala robes, they outrivalled all others in brilliancy at the gay Courts of the French monarchs, as is evident from the contemporary costumes that have escaped the ravages of time. They were popular chiefly about the middle of the sixteenth century.

These samples are all from our own collection.

RENAISSANCE.

Ch. Kreutzberger del _ Régamey lith.

Imp. Lemercier & Cᵗᵉ rue de Seine 57 Paris

XXIX.

SIXTEENTH CENTURY.

EMBROIDERY.

APPLIQUÉ WORK.

THIS magnificent tablecloth, of such a marvellously finished design and so rich in details, that it becomes simply impossible to estimate its endless ornamental motives, is executed on a white satin ground. The design, in black velvet, is obtained by an appliqué process similar to that of the state bed, on Plate XXVII.

This cloth is further embellished with embroideries, with the needle, in red and blue. M. Escosura is its fortunate owner.

Ch Kreutzberger del   Régamey lith

Imp Lemercier & Cie rue de Seine 57 Paris

XXX.

SIXTEENTH CENTURY.

SPANISH EMBROIDERIES.

RENAISSANCE.

Moorish influence disappears nearly altogether from the compositions executed by the Spanish embroiderers. The examples here given—all from our own collection—are partly from the collars of Spanish dalmaticas. Such are the piece at the top of the page and the three others bordering its lower parts. The two remaining ones are ornamented mountings on red ground with gold design.

In the middle is a rich decorative panel, and below it a running pattern in five colours. All these motives are cut out in coloured silks and braided on.

Ch. Kreutzberger del. _ Régamey lith.

Imp. Lemercier & Cⁱᵉ rue de Seine 57 Paris

XXXI.

SIXTEENTH CENTURY.

VELVETS.

BOUND BRANCH PATTERN.

THE bound branch appears as a motive during the second half of this century, and about 1680 is frequently met with in the paintings and tapestries representing persons of rank at this time.

In the middle of our Plate is a splendid sample of green and white velvet on gold ground. The two branches ending in flowers are seen bound together in the centre of the design, which is the usual form adopted in this type. The other examples here given are merely different interpretations of the same idea. We may, however, direct attention to that in the right corner below—red design on gold ground—which, in the lower part of the figure, shows the rudimental broken branch whence spring the various shoots attached together by the central band, a detail which renders it all but certain that this design was executed, if not at the same time, at least not very much later than the lopped branch pattern already spoken of.

RENAISSANCE

Ch Kreutzberger del — Régamey lith.

Imp. Lemercier & Cie rue de Seine 57 Paris

XXXII.

SIXTEENTH CENTURY.

SILKS.

PATTERNS OF FLOWERS DISPOSED IN OPPOSITE DIRECTIONS.

THE close of the sixteenth century offers a far greater variety of types than the foregoing periods, whether this is to be attributed to a greater wealth of ideas amongst artists, or to greater fickleness in the fashions. In any case, this floral type, being always the same wherever it occurs, in velvets, brocade, or damask, need not be subdivided into various special classes. It is constantly repeated in rows of flowrets disposed in horizontal lines. The flowers are so arranged that they all turn to the right in the first row, to the left in the second, and so on.

The four samples in the upper part of our Plate are copies of silk fabrics. The first—yellow design on green ground—is a damask; the three others are interwoven with gold or silver thread.

The four remaining pieces are velvets on gold ground.

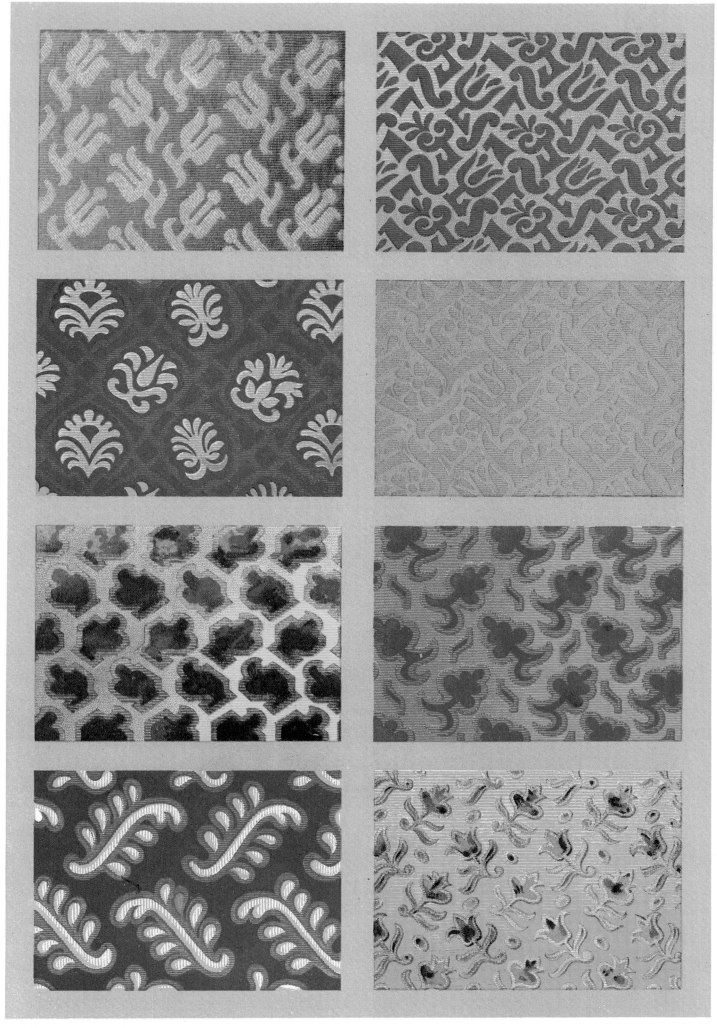

Ch Kreutzberger del. . Régamey lith.

Imp Lemercier & Cie rue de Seine 57 Paris

XXXIII.

SIXTEENTH CENTURY.

SUSPENDED FLORAL PATTERNS.

THIS type, owing to the geometrical disposition of its design, mostly presents a modification of the mullion pattern, while its central motives also bring it into relation with other floral designs already described. For the study of its classification it is important to observe all the minor details. Of three given specimens, two simple and one compound, this last will always be older than the others, whence, in fact, it invariably derives.

The specimen in yellow and red colours, occupying the left of the three central pieces, and that on gold ground next to it, clearly reproduce the mullion form. In the others the prevailing flower work renders its outline less distinct, though easily traced in thought amidst the surrounding details.

All these pieces date from the close of the sixteenth century, though some of them may perhaps be referred to the beginning of the next.

Ch. Kreutzberger del _ Régamey lith

Imp. Lemercier & Cᶦᵉ rue de Seine 57 Paris

XXXIV.

SEVENTEENTH CENTURY.

SILKS.

SPIRAL SCROLL PATTERNS.

WITH the opening of the sixteenth century the Renaissance, abandoning the so-called Gothic style, revived classic art and borrowed its models from it. Thus reappeared those acanthus volutes which Athens and Corinth delighted to see traced on the friezes and capitals of their monuments, and which now began to cover all the secular and religious buildings in Europe.

The artistic designers of ornamental textiles alone resisted the general contagion, long refusing to adopt this motive in their patterns. Doubtless this was partly owing to the prevailing taste for small designs during the second period of the Renaissance, so that it did not begin to be employed till the end of the sixteenth and beginning of the seventeenth century, that is, at the very time when its exaggerated use elsewhere had caused it to degenerate into a vulgar and commonplace stock subject.

Still, the ornamental textile art was less affected than any others by this corruption of taste, and our five specimens, all either pure or modified types of the volute, produce a rich effect, and are perfectly harmonious in their details. The central piece is velvet on full gold ground; that in the upper left corner, silk interwoven with gold; the two lower specimens of a similar description; and that in the right corner, above, a simple green damask on green ground.

XXXV.

SEVENTEENTH CENTURY.

SILKS (ITALY).

PATTERNS OF IRREGULAR AND SERPENTINE LINES.

THE type we here wish to specify, a sort of confused linear imbroglio, scarcely admitting of analysis, without definite design, and accordingly very difficult to name, is nevertheless a Venetian creation of this period, effected by taking here and there incoherent Chinese motives, and executing them in an extremely rich manner. Here the full gold or silver portions conceal the poverty of design, by restricting its play to a simple effect of colour, breaking or relieving the metal by a happy contrast of tones.

Notwithstanding its richness, this type did not seem worthy to occupy one of our Plates all to itself. One of its agreeable effects will be seen in the red and gold specimen in the left corner, below; while that in the right corner, above, shows motives of the lace-work type, contrasting favourably with it. Its neighbour on the left, gold and silver design on grey ground, combines lace motives and those of the serpentine with the irregular lines. Lastly, the fourth specimen, on green, gets rid of all this confusion, creating a new type of serpentine stripes.

All these blendings of motives point at periods coming very close to each other, though somewhat difficult more exactly to determine.

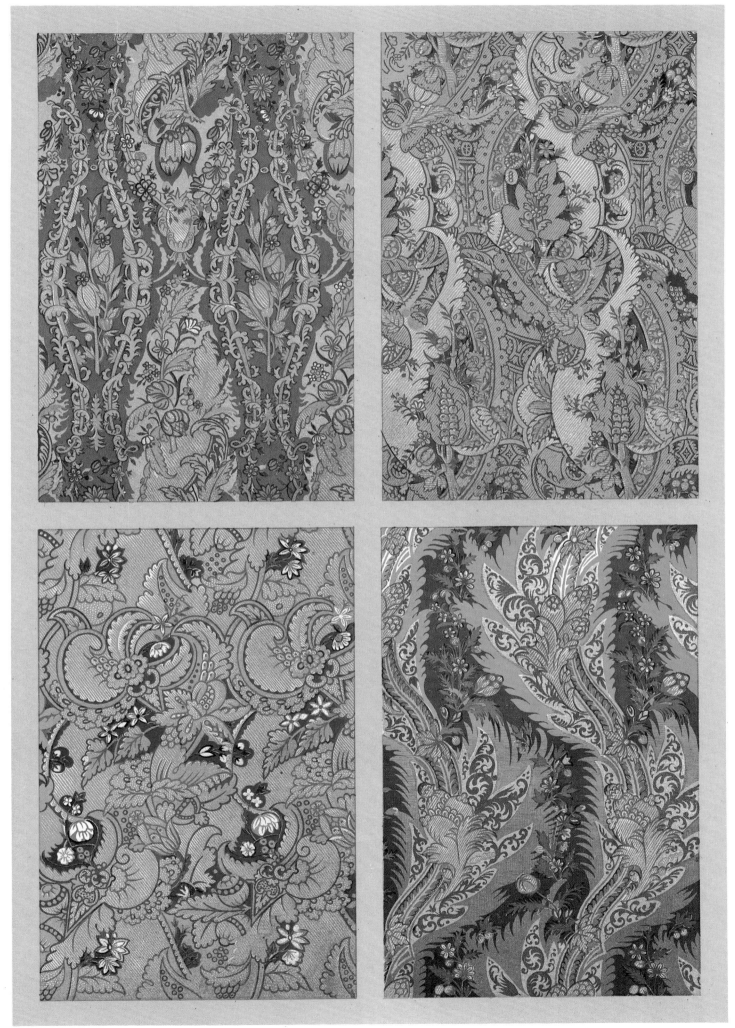

Ch. Kreutzberger del.   Régamey, Lith.

Imp. Bachelin Deflorenne, 13, rue Cassette, Paris

XXXVI.

SEVENTEENTH CENTURY.

SILKS.

PATTERNS OF BRANCHES TWINING IN MULLION FORMS.

THE mullion occurs so frequently in the decoration of textiles that it may be said to have been popular in all ages; this very popularity obliging it to have ever recourse to fresh devices in order to preserve its undying vitality. The fresh combinations it assumed at each period of its revival also mark the precise dates of such successive changes.

The variety here classified belongs, in its foliage and flowers, to the *branch* type, and in the form of its curves to that of the *mullion*. We have accordingly introduced both of these genera into our descriptive title.

The fabric itself presents essential and marked differences from the other specimens of the same decorative character, thus forming a type of its own. Soft as the material of silk handkerchiefs, delicately designed and figured on a satin ground, it forms one of the most remarkable specialities of French manufacture in the seventeenth century.

Our Plate shows four examples of this somewhat rare type, the richest of which—gold designs on green ground—in the upper left corner, has been lent us by its owner, M. Ch. Vail.

Ch. Kreutzberger del.   Régamey lith.   Imp. Rachehn Deflorenne, 13, rue Cassette, Paris.

XXXVII.

SEVENTEENTH CENTURY.

SILKS.

CHINESE IMITATIONS.—VENICE AND LYONS.

DURING the first half of the seventeenth century the commercial relations of the West with China assumed a more important and regular character, and the market of Venice especially was flooded with the fabrics of the extreme East. The taste thus spread for these wares, as is ever the case with rare and uncommon things, soon caused the demand to exceed the supply, thus compelling manufacturers to adapt their looms to the imitation of Chinese designs.

But while the Chinese origin of our six specimens is unmistakable, they seem all to have undergone some slight modification in their disposition, adapting them more to the taste of the West, where such rich figured damasks soon came into general use.

These materials were mostly manufactured in Venice, though Lyons also seems to have had some share in their production; and the last specimen, in the right corner, below, is in any case undoubtedly of French workmanship.

XVIIE SIÈCLE

XXXVIII.

SEVENTEENTH CENTURY.

SILKS.

MANY-COLOURED FLOWER-BED PATTERNS.

THESE vivid many-coloured materials, usually known as *jardinière* or *à parterre*, or, as we might say, "flower-bed patterns," on account of the number of flowers entering into the design, seem to need some more expressive word to determine their type, and we have for this purpose introduced the term "many-coloured" into our title.

These fabrics were in use for dress and hangings during the seventeenth century, the silks being employed for the former, and velvets for the latter purpose. They covered the walls, or decorated those Italian high-backed chairs covered with carvings, or those of a better and simpler taste, common in France during the first period of the reign of Louis XIV. The looms of Lyons competed with those of Italy in their production, and even then the superiority of the French taste is conspicuous in the harmony of the colours and the general disposition of the whole.

Of this type our Plate shows five varieties : two in silk, and three in velvet.

The two damasks, interwoven with gold, are at the head of the page ; the three velvets in the middle and below. They may be generally described as *very effective fabrics.*

Ch. Kreutzberger, del. Regamey, Lith.   Imp. Bachelin-Deflorenne, 13, rue Gassette, Paris.

XXXIX.

SEVENTEENTH CENTURY.

SILKS.

VASE PATTERNS.

THE vase, employed in the decoration of textiles at least so early as the close of the fourteenth century, had regained its ascendency towards the year 1525, and was one of the decorative elements in most general use during the Renaissance. After again falling into disrepute, it was revived by the French artists of the reign of Louis XIV., who employed it for the embellishment of an important series of figured Lyons damasks. It is needless to say that in each successive period it assumed special and characteristic forms ; and we see it here composed of curved rims, fluted body and stem, fashioned after the manner of the works of the goldsmiths' art designed by Lepautre. This remained till the present time the last typical expression of the vase, and occurs only casually in the form of the Greek vases during the Louis XIV. period and the early years of the first empire.

Our five samples are all silk damasks, some interwoven with gold, others with silk, and are all of Lyons workmanship.

XVIIᴱ SIECLE

Ch. Kreutzberger del _ Régamey lith

Imp. Lemercier.& Cᵗᵉ rue de Seine 57 Paris

XL.

SEVENTEENTH CENTURY.

SILKS (FRANCE).

FLOWERED LACE PATTERNS.

AMONGST the various transformations undergone by the lace type, or rather by the design characterizing it, there are some clearly betraying the first symptoms of decline. Such is the type here reproduced, where the fruits or flowers, scattered about isolatedly and in vertical lines, are on the borders alone accompanied by a strip of lace, such as is distinctly seen in the specimen—pink design on green ground—in the right corner below, and where we also see in the centre of the diamond reticulated motive the class of fruit conventionally known as the pomegranate.

In the opposite corner is another piece, where the green and red tones are traced on a black ground. Here the flowers strewn isolatedly on the border, in the central part, are complicated with surroundings of flowered and leafy branches, surmounted and terminated by slender boughs, also furnished with flowers. The pomegranate on the one hand, and on the other the arrangement here described, presently developed into new styles. One step farther and we shall see a type of pomegranate re-appear, adapted to the taste of the seventeenth century, and which will again recover the popularity it had so long ceased to enjoy.

The four remaining specimens, like the two already described, are damasks, interwoven with silk or gold, presenting varied studies of the same pattern.

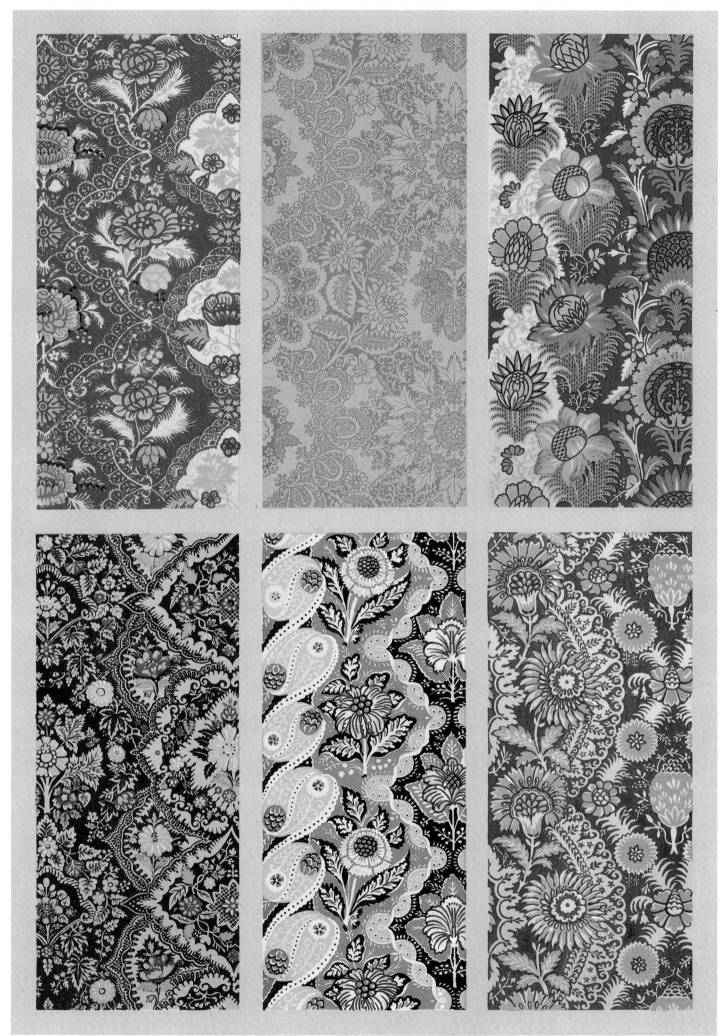

Ch. Kreutzberger del.   Régamey, Lith.   Imp. Bachelin-Deflorenne, 13, rue Cassette, Paris.

XLI.

SEVENTEENTH CENTURY.

SILKS (FRANCE).

LACE PATTERNS.

THIS Plate is so arranged as to further illustrate the statement elsewhere advanced by us, to the effect that the lace pattern never makes its appearance till the latter part of the seventeenth century, contrary to the generally received opinion referring it to the reign of Louis XIII. We may add that a large number of engravings in the National Library, at Paris, reproduce this type as in use at the period in question, for Court costumes of both sexes.

All our samples are brocades, in silk or gold. The most characteristic is that in the right corner, below, on a violet ground, where the lace pattern is seen more distinctly than in any of the others. We may also notice the middle piece, above, showing the shell pattern, so frequently employed by Bérain at this time.

Imp. Rachelin-Deflorenne, 13, rue Cassette, Paris

XLII.

SEVENTEENTH CENTURY.

SILKS.

LACE PATTERNS.

BEFORE quite ceasing to be fashionable, the lace patterns came to be employed for serpentine borders and stripes in appliqué on full materials.

The first sample to the left, above, shows a border of the lace pattern; the flowers in the centre of the design belonging already to the type by which it was soon to be superseded.

In the left corner, below, the serpentine line, with its small lace design, marks a transition stage, the successor to which is foreshadowed by the flowers in the centre.

The two other specimens are, if possible, still more characteristic of this mixed period, which we shall see soon replaced by stripes of various sorts and festoons.

XLIII.

SEVENTEENTH CENTURY.

PATTERNS OF BIRDS PERCHED AND ON THE WING.

BIRDS were employed in the seventeenth century to enliven and fill in the spaces left empty by the bunches of flowers or twining and flowering plants used in the embellishments of textiles at this period. They are evidently of Chinese and Japanese origin, having been copied from porcelain or lacquered ware.

The Japanese or Chinese taste is especially obvious in the specimen to the left, above, on our Plate, while in the other three it betrays unmistakable proofs of having been modified by the influence of French ideas. They are all silks, damasks, or satins, of Lyons workmanship, in our collection.

Ch Kreutzberger del _ Régamey lith   Imp Lemercier & Cie rue de Seine 57 Paris

XLIV.

SEVENTEENTH CENTURY.

FLAT EMBROIDERY.

THE original pieces composing this Plate belong to the second half of this century. They are conceived quite in the French taste, as more particularly typified by Bérain.

They are skilfully embroidered *on the surface alone* by means of very fine gold and silver threads.

The two borders at top of the sheet are on drab grounds. The blue silk in the centre is adorned with the emblem of the sun, encircled by various ornamental details. It is flanked on either side by two panels on pink silk, and surmounted by the border of a chalice cover on crimson silk.

Below is a cloth of red silk, showing its border, the inner portion being filled in with flowrets in alternating designs.

44

XVIIᴱ SIÈCLE

Imp Lemercier & Cⁱᵉ rue de Seine 57 Paris

XLV.

FROM THE TWELFTH TO THE SEVENTEENTH CENTURY.

PASSEMENTERIES (GIMPS AND FRINGES).

VARIOUS PATTERNS.

PASSEMENTERIE may be looked on as the necessary complement of the ornamental textile art. Hence we cannot but give a place in our collection to the few varieties of galloons, borders, or fringes, more usually employed during the course of several centuries.

The various subdivisions of our Plate will readily give an idea of the general character of this description of ornaments. The middle piece at the top of the page is a border woven with silver on a red silk. The process employed in its manufacture, and the Byzantine form of the design, enable us unhesitatingly to refer it to the close of the twelfth century.

The two smaller borders, the diamond pattern of which is worked in the same way, one silver and red silk, the other silver and gold coloured silk, right and left of the third line, must be assigned to the same period.

At the extremities of the first line are: on the left, a green fringe in coarse silk (gros grain), adorning a fabric of the fourteenth century; on the right, a fringe in three colours, green, yellow, and red, equally distributed, found on a material similar to the foregoing.

Two very beautiful plaited fringes occupy the centre of the third and fourth lines. They date from the fifteenth and beginning of the sixteenth century, and vividly recall the lace patterns then in vogue.

In the second row we see, right and left, two interlaced or knotted fringes, richer than the previous; one red and gold, the other blue and silver; also in general use during the sixteenth century.

The fifth and sixth lines are occupied with curtain bands, dating from the beginning of the seventeenth century, the two ends of which are joined by means of the olive button, in our Illustration appearing below the loop.

Lastly, two specimens of passementerie, as fancy fastenings for articles of dress—one in the second line, blue and gold, the other in the fourth, red and gold on imitation gold brocade—belong to the sixteenth century. Between the loop and the olive button of the last is a little specimen of a border, gold and red silk, also of the sixteenth century.

45

XVᴱ XVIᴱ XVIIᴱ SIÈCLE

Ch Kreutzberger del _ Régamey lith

Imp. Lemercier & Cⁱᵉ rue de Seine 57 Paris

XLVI.

EIGHTEENTH CENTURY.

FIGURED DAMASKS.

TWINING RIBBON PATTERNS "À RÉSERVES."

THE twining ribbon pattern *à réserve*, and encircling flowers within their spiral volutions, were amongst the most popular products of the Lyons factories at the close of the seventeenth century. The specimens here given are chosen from a large number of similar materials, preference being accorded to such as presented either greater variety or greater richness in their designs.

The damask interwoven with gold on a white ground, in the left corner, above, is more elegant and more learnedly designed than the other on violet ground adjoining it, which, though richer, seems to produce a heavier decorative effect.

In the sample on red ground, we may remark on the ribbon fancy work, reproducing the exact designs of the ribbons manufactured about the same time. Lastly, we have thought it desirable to contrast this with another of the same type, in which the ribbon pattern is seen replaced by a twining branch of flowers.

Ch. Kreutzberger del. _ Régamey lith   Imp Lemercier & Cⁱᵉ rue de Seine 57 Paris

XLVII.

EIGHTEENTH CENTURY.

SILKS.

RIBBON AND SERPENTINE STRIPE PATTERNS.

THE painter, Louis Tocqué (ob. 1772), in his portrait of Marie Leckzinska, wife of Louis XV., painted in 1740, enables us to fix the date when the type here described became fashionable. In the picture the Queen is represented standing, and dressed in a robe designed with flowering poppies entwined in golden ornaments, in the manner of the six specimens on our Plate. In a critique of this portrait the late M. Frédéric Villot remarks that the artist "has reproduced with rare skill the brilliancy of the gold and silver stuffs, as well as the lustre of the flowered satins and the embroidery."

So true is this, that even an observer but little familiar with the various fabrics will at once recognise in the Queen's robe a white satin interwoven with gold and various colours, manufactured in the style for which the Lyons factories were then, as now, justly celebrated.

After this, no further analysis will be needed of a Plate which merely furnishes so many varieties of a somewhat uniform type.

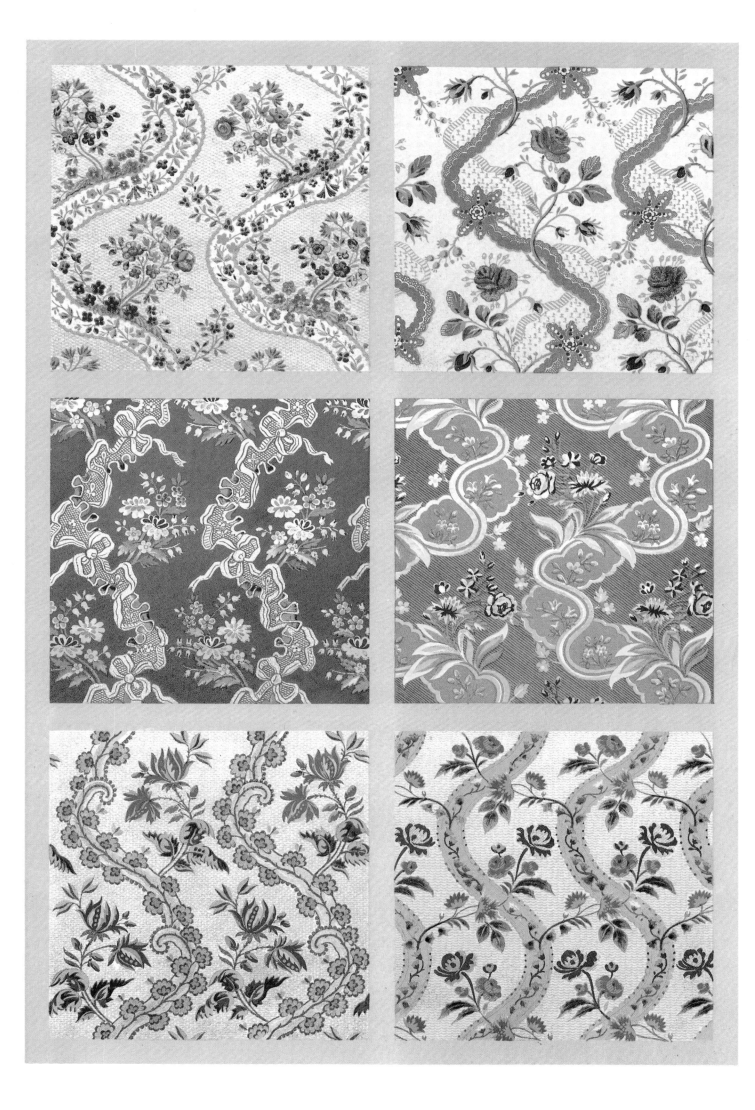

XLVIII.

EIGHTEENTH CENTURY.

SILKS.

ENTWINED RIBBON PATTERNS.

THIS type is more generally allied to the *medallion* pattern, which it at times replaces by means of ingenious loopings. The graceful convolutions of the ribbon, form of themselves a sufficient framework for the flowers or trophies occupying the space thus left vacant.

The portraits of Louis XVI. and of Marie Antoinette, printed on white satin at top of our Plate, enable us to assign a more definite date to the other specimens here reproduced. They all belong so uniformly to the same type that a detailed analysis of each may be dispensed with. It will be enough to add that Philibert de la Salle designed the greater part of these compositions for the Lyons mills.

To the Marquis de Selve's courtesy we are indebted for the opportunity afforded us of adorning our work with the above-mentioned portraits of Louis XVI. and his Queen.

Ch Kreutzberger del   Régamey lith

Imp. Lemercier & Cie rue de Seine 57 Paris

XLIX.

EIGHTEENTH CENTURY.

SILKS, SATINS, AND DAMASKS.

TWINING BRANCH AND SERPENTINE PATTERNS.

THE eighteenth century, while retaining the motive of branches with leaves and flowers disposed in serpentine lines, impoverished them to such an extent as to impart to them quite a different character from the corresponding type of previous epochs. To this character was superadded another, consisting in breaking the regularity of the vertical serpentine lines, and scattering the fragments erratically, while so disposing the bunches of flowers and the foliage as to make them fill up the empty spaces of the design.

From this practice arose the *serpentines*, and the types in the lower left corner of our Plate, where we see them in red and green, accompanied by red roses, filling in the vacant spaces, as above explained.

At the top of the sheet are two analogous dispositions, of which that to the left is produced by the combination of both types.

The three remaining specimens are all figured satins, where the waving line, whether broken or regular, is the essential element.

This description of textiles must be referred to about the year 1775.

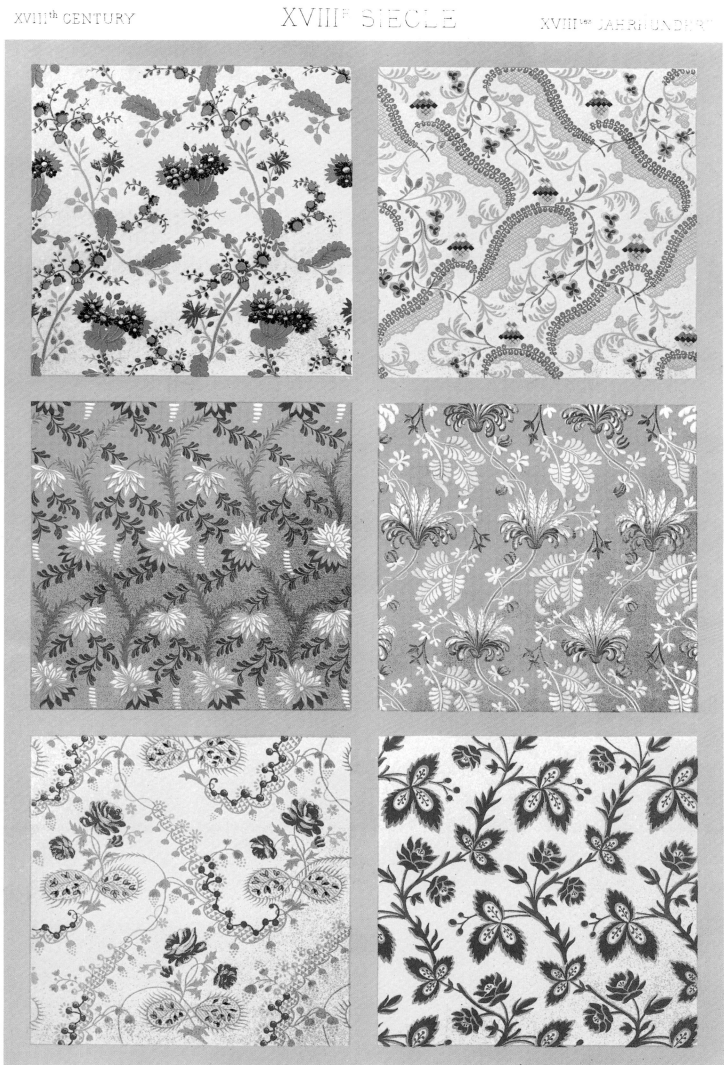

L.

EIGHTEENTH CENTURY.

SILKS (FRANCE).

STRAIGHT STRIPE PATTERNS.

THIS type, various forms of which occupy our Plate, belongs to the latter half of the eighteenth century, a period when the public, distracted by the political throes of the times, turned their attention from art subjects. These simple stripes, artlessly strewn with flowrets, appeared towards the last years of Louis XVI., and were retained during the Republic and the Consulate. The artistic industries of the times already felt that rich tissues were no longer in harmony with the surroundings, and that social convulsions are but sorry foster-mothers of true art, banishing to a foreign soil both artist and artisan, and in the place of the glorious conquests, toilsomely acquired during the course of ages of labour, bringing about a partial return to barbarism.

Our specimens call for no detailed comments, all belonging to a general type, whose varieties are simple in themselves and easily grasped.

Ch. Kreutzberger, del.   Régamey, Lith.   Imp. Bachelin-Deflorenne, 13, rue Cassette, Paris.

CONTENTS.

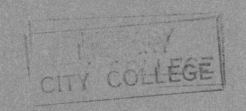